MELBOURNE
ENCOUNTER

JAYNE D'ARCY
DONNA WHEELER

Melbourne Encounter

Published by Lonely Planet Publications Pty Ltd
ABN 36 005 607 983

Australia (Head Office)	Locked Bag 1, Footscray, Vic 3011 ☎ 03 8379 8000 fax 03 8379 8111
USA	150 Linden St, Oakland, CA 94607 ☎ 510 250 6400 toll free 800 275 8555 fax 510 893 8572
UK	2nd fl, 186 City Rd London EC1V 2NT ☎ 020 7106 2100 fax 020 7106 2101
Contact	talk2us@lonelyplanet.com lonelyplanet.com/contact

The 1st edition of Lonely Planet's *Melbourne Encounter* was written and researched by Donna Wheeler. This title was commissioned in Lonely Planet's Melbourne office and produced by: **Commissioning Editor** Maryanne Netto **Coordinating Editor** Victoria Harrison **Coordinating Cartographer** Xavier Di Toro **Coordinating Layout Designer** Wibowo Rusli **Senior Editor** Susan Paterson **Managing Editor** Kirsten Rawlings **Managing Cartographer** David Connolly **Managing Layout Designer** Jane Hart **Assisting Editor** Gabrielle Innes **Cover Research** Naomi Parker **Internal Image Research** Rebecca Skinner **Thanks to** Annelies Mertens, Marg Toohey

Cover photograph Diners and pedestrians in Centre Place, Glenn Beanland/Lonely Planet Images.

All images are copyright of the photographers unless otherwise indicated. Many of the images in this guide are available for licensing from Lonely Planet Images: lonelyplanetimages.com

10 9 8 7 6 5 4 3 2 1   2nd edition
ISBN: 978 1 74179 563 9   Printed in China

HOW TO USE THIS BOOK
Colour-Coding & Maps

Colour-coding is used for symbols on maps and in the text that they relate to (eg all eating venues on the maps and in the text are given a green knife and fork symbol). Each neighbourhood also gets its own colour, and this is used down the edge of the page and throughout that neighbourhood section.

Shaded yellow areas on the maps denote areas of interest – for their historical significance, their attractive architecture or their great bars and restaurants. We encourage you to head to these areas and just start exploring!

Send us your feedback We love to hear from travellers – your comments keep us on our toes and help make our books better. Our well-travelled team reads every word on what you loved or loathed about this book. Although we cannot reply individually to postal submissions, we always guarantee that your feedback goes straight to the appropriate authors, in time for the next edition. Each person who sends us information is thanked in the next edition, and the most useful submissions are rewarded with a free book.

Visit **lonelyplanet.com** to submit your updates and suggestions or to ask for help. Our award-winning website also features inspirational travel stories, news and discussions.

Note: We may edit, reproduce and incorporate your comments in Lonely Planet products such as guidebooks, websites and digital products, so let us know if you don't want your comments reproduced or your name acknowledged. For a copy of our privacy policy visit lonelyplanet.com/privacy.

JAYNE D'ARCY

Growing up in the Melbourne seaside suburb of Frankston had its advantages for Jayne; it motivated her to catch the train from the outer suburbs into the inner city to hang out in Prahran's Greville St, Fitzroy's Brunswick St, St Kilda and the Queen Vic market. She hit 18 and swapped countries before returning to make the Great Ocean Road her home while she studied journalism. After a long-ish spell working in community radio in Timor-Leste, she finally settled with her family in Melbourne's vibrant north (in Zone 1, just). When she's not riding her French 1970s folding bike around North Fitzroy, booking flights or pretending to renovate, Jayne is a freelance writer.

JAYNE'S THANKS

Thanks Maryanne Netto at Lonely Planet for letting me delve so deeply into Melbourne. Thanks to Jane O'Neill and Dave Carswell who share a love of the city. Thanks Sharik Billington for your amazing support and our grade-one boy, Miles, who loves researching restaurants just as much as I do.

Our readers Many thanks to the travellers who wrote to us with helpful hints, useful advice and interesting anecdotes.

The bike-friendly sculptural Webb Bridge, inspired by Koorie fishing traps, Docklands (p54)

CONTENTS

>THIS IS MELBOURNE

Melbourne is a city you need to get to know. It won't take your breath away with overtly seductive geography on first sight. Its many charms aren't always immediately apparent on first meeting. But there's no doubt this city will get under your skin.

Few cities grew as fast and furiously as this one, and it launched itself onto the world stage with an arriviste swagger and a gold-tinted twinkle in its eye. With its Victorian streetscapes and genteel demeanour, Melbourne was considered the most British of Australian cities. These days, it possesses both an adopted European grace and a nonstop energy more akin to the urban hubs of Asia. Melbourne's citizens look as diverse as they are. It's a city of immigrants whose backgrounds usually span multiple ethnicities. They're good-looking too, though that can often be down to culture as much as nature. They'd rather appear effortlessly interesting than 'done'. Its mood could be considered serious, but that's softened by a sensuality uncommon in Australian cities. People aren't afraid to look each other in the eye, to appreciate details. Street life here has a sexy, celebratory edge. Melburnians are passionate about enjoying life: food, fashion, sport and socialising are cherished. Its many bars, cafes and restaurants draw on the best from Europe, Asia and the Middle East, while retaining an easy-going quintessentially Australian feel. Melbourne, like its city laneways, is many-layered and full of surprises. It's industrious, imaginative and creative; prolific in architecture, performance, live music and the visual arts but also endlessly self-deprecating. It's one of the world's youngest cities yet also one of the longest inhabited places on earth. It's resolutely urbane and irrevocably suburban. Life buzzes in its often beautifully designed interior spaces, though it's also outdoorsy, with a wealth of parks and close proximity to beaches and the bush. It's car-centric but totally devoted to its trams. It can be complicated, cliquey and cultish, then warm, welcoming and generous.

Melbourne is a city worth exploring: let it win you over.

Top left View over the wave-roofed Southern Cross Station **Top right** Leisurely stroll along the foreshore at St Kilda (p112) **Bottom** Time for cafe culture, Degraves St (p10)

> HIGHLIGHTS

JAMES BRAUND / LONELY PLANET IMAGES ©
Melbourne's renowned laneways bustle with life

>1 LANEWAYS

EXPLORE THE CITY'S LABYRINTHINE LANEWAYS

Between Melbourne's grid of wide, dignified main streets lies an enticing network of lanes, passageways and arcades. These laneways and 'little' streets were a happy accident. Not part of city designer Robert Hoddle's grand vision, they came into being firstly as service lanes. The hunger for real estate then saw them fronted with shops, warehouses and residences, and the tale of two cities began.

Although they've always bustled with commerce (and in some cases, vice), the laneways have only taken on a life of their own within the last 20 years. Join the constant eddy of crowds who come to pick up a pair of Swedish jeans, mingle at a gallery opening, eat a plate of *bacala* (salt cod) fritters or sip a vodka and elderflower.

Start with the big lanes and little streets: Flinders Lane, Little Bourke St and Little Collins St. Most of the action happens east of Queen St and continues right up to Spring St. From Flinders, a warehouse-lined strip once devoted to *schmate* business (the Jewish rag trade), you'll find Degraves St, Centre Way and Manchester Lane; Hosier Lane, Oliver Lane and Duckboard Place; and Bligh Place and Bond St. From Little Collins (the 'Littles' often lose their 'street' suffix in conversation) you can wander through the Block or Royal Arcades, Meyers Place and Gills Lane. Little Bourke's attendant lanes run off to the left and to the right. The residents range from edgy hidden bars, such as Berlin Bar (p48), Roxanne Parlour (p52) and the Croft Institute (www.thecroftinstitute.com.au; 21–25 Croft Alley), to the Flower Drum (17 Market Lane), one of the city's most acclaimed restaurants. Crossley St, at the Spring St end, is particularly vibrant with Italian restaurant Becco (www.becco.com.au) and a unique collection of shops and bars. Explore: the sense of discovery is part of the experience.

Apart from the life that goes on in them, the laneways have become an attraction for their very walls and surfaces, which are often covered in the dreams, imaginings and obsessions of Melbourne artists. Tagging, stencils and large loopy designs more akin to illustration go far beyond the idea of graffiti. Melbourne City Council, despite some slip-ups (including recently painting over what appeared to be a Banksy), has generally embraced the city's 'street art capital of the world' status. Artists are invited to do their thing in designated art zones (an irony not

WIBOWO RUSLI

lost on the artists and not something that has stopped stencils gracing unsanctified walls). These colourful and densely decorated passages include Hosier Lane, Croft Alley, Duckboard Place and Union Lane. The annual Laneways Commission (www.melbourne.vic.gov.au) also invites artists to install work in unexpected places, and the City Lights Project (www.citylightsproject.com), just off Centre Place, curates shows in il-luminated boxes that shine 24/7.

>2 IAN POTTER CENTRE: NGV AUSTRALIA

GET UP CLOSE WITH AUSTRALIAN ART

The Ian Potter Centre was designed as a showcase for the National Gallery of Victoria's extensive collection of Australian paintings, decorative arts, photography, prints, drawings, sculpture, fashion, textiles and jewellery. An integral part of the Federation Sq development, the gallery opened its doors in 2002, becoming the first public art museum dedicated entirely to Australian art. The building is entered via an atrium designed to evoke the great galleries of Europe, its many fractured panes at the same time referencing the city's own ever-dissecting grid. Once inside, the building's use of glass makes visitors feel as if they are part of the display, as well as splicing city vignettes into the architecture: rail yards, the loopy turrets of the Forum Theatre (see p53), the green expanses of garden across the river.

The gallery's Indigenous Collection dominates the ground floor; the collection is given a central position often denied to Aboriginal art in institutions and seeks to challenge ideas of the 'authentic'. There are some particularly fine examples of Papunya painting, such as the epic *Napperby Death Spirit Dreaming* (1980) by Clifford Possum Tjapaltjarri and Tim Leura Tjapaltjarri. Brook Andrew's *Gun Metal Grey* (2007) series, which makes use of ethnographic photographs of unidentified 19th-century Aborigines, is viscerally haunting, almost unbearably so.

Upstairs, there are permanent displays of colonial paintings and some unmissable drawings by 19th-century Aboriginal artists William Barack and Tommy McCrae. There's also the work of Heidelberg School impressionists including Tom Roberts, Frederick McCubbin and Arthur Streeton. Streeton's *Spring* (Heidelberg, 1890) encapsulates the plein-air techniques and obsession with local light and landscape that the school is known for, while McCubbin's *The Pioneer* (Mt Macedon, 1904) depicts a quintessential Australian story. There is an extensive collection of the work of the modernist 'Angry Penguins', including Sir Sidney Nolan, Arthur Boyd, Joy Hester and Albert Tucker. John Perceval's *Soul Singer, Luna Park* (1942–3) is an amazing example of this group's dark depictions of wartime Melbourne. Nolan's *Dimboola* series and his paintings *Footballer* and *Bathers*, of the same period, are iconic.

DANIEL MAHON

John Brack's *Collins St 5pm* (1955) is an evocative rendering of midcentury city life and is joined by the work of socialist realist Noel Counihan, Ian Fairweather and landscape painter Fred Williams.

The permanent collection has some fabulous examples of the work of local midcareer artists such as Jenny Watson, Bill Henson, Tony Clark and Gordon Bennett. The next generation are more often represented in temporary exhibitions, though you can catch a sculptural work by Patricia Piccinini – the unsettling anthropomorphic *Nest* (2006) – in its permanent collection. It's a pity that the 150 works of the Joseph Brown collection (some great, others so very so-so) hog permanent space that could have housed an up-to-the-minute snapshot of Melbourne's contemporary works, but such are the vicissitudes of philanthropy. See p38 for more details.

>3 AUSTRALIAN RULES FOOTBALL

SEE THE BIG MEN FLY AT THE MCG DURING FOOTY SEASON

Ah, the footy. Visit Melbourne from around the end of March to the last weekend in September and you'll find the AFL (Australian Football League) hard to ignore. Make it to a match at the Melbourne Cricket Ground (MCG; p81) and you might just fall in love. The game of football is known for its cracking pace, aerial grabs, long-shot goals, intense physicality and athleticism. At its best, high-scoring action keeps the crowd engaged and in full voice from beginning to end. The MCG, affectionately referred to as the 'G', has been the home of football since 1859, and its atmosphere can't be replicated.

The AFL may now have teams in every mainland state but nine of its 17 clubs are still based in Melbourne. Since the demise of the local grounds, all of these teams play their home games at either the MCG or Docklands Stadium; the current MCG tenant clubs are Melbourne, Richmond, Collingwood and Hawthorn. Games between two Melbourne teams ensure a loud, parochial crowd. Games are held on Friday or Saturday night, as well as Saturday or Sunday afternoon. Tickets can be had for surprisingly little compared to Premier League soccer matches or American NFL games, with reserved seats from $38 a pop. Seats in the upper stands ('up with the gulls') can seem a little removed, but if you're on the Punt Rd side of the ground, you'll get the additional thrill of a magnificent city view.

For day games, things start with a ritual walk from Federation Sq. The path through Birrarung Marr is particularly scenic and the excitement mounts as you approach the G. Kick-off is usually just after 2pm. For sustenance, there are meat pies and hot chips at half time. Thirsts are quenched with beer sipped from plastic cups at quarter time and three-quarter time. (A BYO thermos of tea and a sandwich is a perfectly acceptable substitute.)

Barracking is often a one-sided 'conversation' with the umpire (who is usually referred to as 'white maggot', drawn from their once-white uniforms, now just 'maggot' for short). 'Baaallll' is shouted long and loud each time a player is tackled while holding the ball. When the siren blows, and after the winning club theme song is played (usually several times over), it's off to the pub. Supporters of opposing teams often celebrate and commiserate together. Despite the deep tribal feelings and passionate

TOM COCKREM / LONELY PLANET IMAGES ©

expression of belonging that AFL engenders, violence is almost unheard of pre-, post- or during games.

Interestingly enough, women follow football in almost equal numbers as men. It's been hotly debated if this is due to the players' grace and speed, or more to do with their squeakily tight shorts. We'll let you be the umpire on that.

>4 GERTRUDE ST

TAKE STYLE SERIOUSLY IN GERTRUDE ST, MELBOURNE'S NEWEST FASHION HOTSPOT

The Macedonian and Albanian social clubs have moved on, but Melbourne's most freshly hip neighbourhood is not entirely without remnants of its past. Spliced among the peddlers of deconstructed Belgian frocks, rare 12-inch vinyl and mandarin-scented hand creams, stalwarts remain: a secondhand fridge shop, the Aboriginal community gym that trained boxing great Lionel Rose, habit-clad nuns, residents of rooming houses and public-housing tower blocks. As recently as the early '90s it was a street that didn't lend itself to casual evening strolls; there were pubs where it was rumoured you could 'get jobs done', and we're not talking lawn mowing or paving. The stark contrast of affluence and disadvantage can still unsettle, but there's a mitigating energy and a relaxing, welcoming vibe. Yes, it's now undeniably cool, but it still feels like a community.

Close to the Royal Exhibition Building (p105), the southern side of the road is dominated by St Vincent's hospital services, while the other side has handmade pioneers Little Salon (No 71) and Cottage Industry (No 67), as well as the cute cafe Radio (No 79) and the Workers Club (corner Gertrude and Brunswick Sts). One of Melbourne's best restaurants, Cutler & Co (p98), is spreading further along Gertrude St, while there's Seven Seeds coffee royalty at De Clieu (No 187). Across Brunswick St there is excellent vintage clothing at Circa Vintage Clothing (No 102) and Moustache (No 124), as well as intriguing furniture and collectibles at South Fitzroy Antiques (No 90) and Max Watt's Industria (No 202). Gertrude St fashion tends towards the cerebral: Left (p93) stocks international heavyweights, locals are represented by Signet Bureau (p94), Nom-D (No 203) and Obüs (No 226). In addition to clothing, Spacecraft (p94) has a collection of botanical and architectural-inspired printed textiles. Frederick Gugenberg (corner Gertrude and Smith Sts) does menswear of the slick, streamlined variety. With delightfully obliging staff, Artisan Books (No 159), which stocks decorative arts monographs, and Books for Cooks (p91) are prime browsing destinations. Title (p92) also has some printed gems, and many covetable CDs and DVD box sets. Food wise, Ladro (p99) should be on any visitor's must-eat list, and there's the Gertrude St Enoteca (p100) and Birdman Eating (p97) for all-day snacks and imbibing.

JAMES BRAUND / LONELY PLANET IMAGES ©

Añada (p96) opens in the evening for tapas. The once rough-as-guts Gertrude Hotel (No 148) and the Builders Arms Hotel (No 211) are now firmly in the hands of the hip, but still manage to be comfortable old boozers if a beer beckons. Aesop (No 242), a luscious local skincare outfit, also has an airy shop to refresh the senses before you hit Smith St. Don't miss the Melbourne bag-staple Crumpler (corner Gertrude and Smith Sts) or smile-inducing odds and ends at Third Drawer Down (p94).

Finally, no Gertrude St stroll would be complete without art. Head to Gertrude Contemporary Art Spaces (p90) and Seventh Gallery (No 155) for some up-and-coming action.

REBECCA SKINNER

>5 ST KILDA

STROLL ST KILDA'S SWEET PROMENADE

St Kilda is no slouch when it comes to entertainment, but a simple stroll around its streets can be as rewarding as a visit to one of its many cafes, restaurants or bars. St Kilda's moods are unpredictable. Come in high summer on a Friday night or Sunday afternoon and you'll discover the celebrity good-time suburb. Find yourself here on a wintery day midweek and you'll feel the full melancholic pangs of a Paul Kelly song (and understand why painters, poets and musicians have chosen to live here).

The long pier that juts from the foreshore is a requisite for romantics; the historic kiosk at its end was destroyed by fire but has now been lovingly reconstructed. The Esplanade takes you along the high road past the Esplanade Hotel (p117), where the views of the bay are splendid, or keep to the shore and feel the sand between your toes. Beyond the beach, there's pretty Catani Gardens to the west and the St Kilda Botanical Gardens tucked away behind Acland St to the east. The wide gravel paths of the gardens invite leisurely walks, and there are plenty of shady spots to sprawl on the lawns. Or check out local indigenous plants, the subtropical rainforest conservatory or the springtime splendour of the rose garden.

>MELBOURNE DIARY

Melbourne isn't fussy about when it gets festive. Winter's chills or summer's swelter offer no excuse, with Melburnians joining like minds at outdoor festivals, in cinemas, performance spaces or sporting venues year-round. Sporting events in particular draw incredibly large crowds; the party often spills out of the stadiums and into the city. Cultural festivals also have enthusiastic audiences, for both the main event and the pre- and after-partying. Summer is celebrated both informally and with festivals that have an obvious emphasis on the outdoors. What follows is a selection; check www.thatsmelbourne.com.au for comprehensive event listings. See p160 for a list of public holidays.

Australian Formula One Grand Prix (p22)

MELBOURNE DIARY

JANUARY

Australian Open
www.australianopen.com
The world's top players and huge merry-making crowds descend on the National Tennis Centre at Melbourne Park (p87) for Australia's Grand Slam tennis championship. Ground passes make for a grand day out if you're not desperate to see a top seed.

Midsumma Festival
www.midsumma.org.au
Melbourne's annual gay and lesbian arts festival features over 100 events from mid-January to mid-February, with a Pride March finale. Expect everything from film screenings to a high-camp rowing regatta, history walks to dance parties.

Big Day Out
www.bigdayout.com
National rock fest comes to town at the end of January. Big names are guaranteed, but the local Lily Pad lads often steal the show.

Chinese New Year
www.melbournechinatown.com.au
Melbourne has celebrated the Chinese lunar New Year since Little Bourke St became Chinatown in the 1860s. The time to touch the dragon falls sometime towards the end of January or early February.

FEBRUARY

St Kilda Festival
www.stkildafestival.com.au
This week-long festival ends in a suburb-wide street party on the final Sunday. The crowds are large and laid-back, if not as uniformly bohemian as they once were.

St Jerome's Laneway Festival
www.lanewayfestival.com.au
Indie kids outgrew their natural laneway habitat and now bump along to new and revered bands beside Footscray's Maribyrnong River. Held at the end of February.

KRZYSZTOF DYDYNSKI / LONELY PLANET IMAGES ©
Celebrating the colour of Chinese New Year

Epicurial exhibitionism at the Melbourne Food & Wine Festival

PHIL WEYMOUTH / LONELY PLANET IMAGES ©

Melbourne Food & Wine Festival

www.melbournefoodandwine.com.au

Market tours, wine tastings, cooking classes and presentations by celebrity chefs take place at venues across the city in February and/or March. Chew the gastronomic fat or just eat your fill.

MARCH

Melbourne Fashion Festival

www.mff.com.au

This week-long style-fest features salon shows and parades showcasing established designers' ranges. Join the air-kiss set or get down with the up-and-comings at one of the many offshoot happenings.

Melbourne Bikefest

www.melbournebikefest.com.au

This annual festival celebrates Melbourne's cycling community over four days.

Melbourne Queer Film Festival

www.mqff.com.au

This long-running film festival features Australian and international queer films at the Australian Centre for the Moving Image.

MELBOURNE DIARY

Veterans proudly march in the Anzac Day Parade

EMMA MCNICOL

Moomba Festival
www.thatsmelbourne.com.au
Moomba has had something of a new millennium makeover, with the action focussed around the Yarra River (Alexandra Gardens and Birrarung Marr). An old favourite is the wacky Birdman Rally, where competitors launch themselves into the river in homemade flying machines.

Australian Formula One Grand Prix
www.grandprix.com.au
The 5.3km street circuit around normally tranquil Albert Park Lake is known for its smooth, fast surface. The buzz, both on the streets and in your ears, takes over Melbourne for four fully sick days of rev-head action.

APRIL

International Comedy Festival
www.comedyfestival.com.au
An enormous range of local and international comic talent hits town with 3½ weeks of stand-up comedy, cabaret, theatre, street performance, film, TV, radio and visual arts.

Melbourne International Flower & Garden Show
www.melbflowershow.com.au
The Royal Exhibition Building and the surrounding Carlton Gardens are taken over by backyard blitzers, DIY-ers and plenty of dotty old ladies.

Anzac Day Parade
www.shrine.org.au
On 25 April, Australians remember the WWI Australian and New Zealand Army Corps

(Anzac) defeat at Gallipoli and honour all those who have served in war with a dawn service at the Shrine of Remembrance, in Kings Domain, and a veterans' parade along St Kilda Rd.

MAY

St Kilda Film Festival

www.stkildafilmfestival.com.au
Australia's first, and arguably best, short-film festival, with a great grab bag of genres and talent on show. Opening night pulls local film-industry stars (dressed down for the occasion, of course).

JUNE

Melbourne International Jazz Festival

www.melbournejazz.com
Venues such as Bennetts Lane jazz club (p51) and the Melbourne Recital Centre are filled with jazz-lovers for the first two weeks of June.

JULY

State of Design Festival

www.stateofdesign.com.au
Twelve days of exhibitions, forums, design shows, workshops and competitions. The Melbourne Design Market (www.melbourne designmarket.com.au) is held at Federation Sq during the festival and in December.

Melbourne International Film Festival

www.miff.com.au
Midwinter brings out black-skivvy-wearing cinephiles in droves. It's held over two weeks in July and August at various cinemas. The music documentary program is a particular treat.

AUGUST

Melbourne Art Fair

www.artfair.com.au
Biennial art-star gathering, with galleries from the Asia-Pacific region setting up shop in the Royal Exhibition Building. Next one is in 2012.

Melbourne Writers Festival

www.mwf.com.au
Beginning in the last week of August, the writers' festival is held at Federation Sq and other venues and features 10 days of forums and events celebrating reading, writing, books and ideas.

SEPTEMBER

AFL Grand Final

www.afl.com.au
It's easier to get a goal from the boundary than to pick up tickets to the grand final at the MCG. But it's not hard to get your share of finals fever. Pubs put on big screens and barbecues (often with a spot of street kick-to-kick at half time). For the truly devoted, there's the Grand Final Parade on the preceding Friday.

Royal Melbourne Show

www.royalshow.com.au

The country comes to town in September and October for this large agricultural fair. Where else do you get to see the woodchop? Held at the Royal Melbourne Showgrounds in Flemington.

Melbourne Fringe Festival

www.melbournefringe.com.au

The Fringe takes place in September and October and showcases experimental theatre, music and visual arts.

OCTOBER & NOVEMBER

Melbourne International Arts Festival

www.melbournefestival.com.au

Held at various venues around the city, the festival features an always thought-provoking program of Australian and international theatre, opera, dance, visual arts and music.

Movember

www.movember.com

Melbourne is where Movember started, so expect more than the usual quota of unshaven men on the streets. It's a fundraiser for men's health.

Spring Racing Carnival

www.springracingcarnival.com.au

Culminating in the prestigious Melbourne Cup at Flemington Racecourse, these

DAWN DELANEY / LONELY PLANET IMAGES ©
The Melbourne Cup carnival is a prestigious affair

race meets are as much social events as sporting ones. The Cup, held on the first Tuesday in November, is a public holiday in Melbourne.

DECEMBER

Boxing Day Test

www.mcg.org.au

Day one of the Boxing Day Test at the MCG draws out the cricket fans. Expect some shenanigans from Bay 13.

New Year's Eve

www.thatsmelbourne.com.au

Fireworks light up the Yarra River at 9pm and midnight.

Life's everything but square at Federation Sq

ITINERARIES

Melbourne's compact city centre and straightforward public transport system make discovering its delights easy to do in a couple of days. Do get your walking shoes on, but resist the urge to over-schedule; Melbourne is at its best when you take it nice and slow and leave time for serendipity.

DAY ONE

Head for the city's laneways, grabbing a coffee on Degraves St. Take in the Ian Potter Centre: National Gallery of Victoria Australia (p38) and the Australian Centre for the Moving Image (p38) at Federation Sq, and then head back up Hosier Lane for a full-frontal, street-art assault. Window-shop your way along Flinders Lane. Head up to Earl Canteen (p45) or grab a lunch box from Café Vue (p48) and picnic on the grass of the Kings Domain. The Royal Botanic Gardens (p71) beckon if the day is fine, otherwise grab a tram back into the city, browse the vertical village of Curtin House (252 Swanston St) then slide into a booth for cocktails at the Toff in Town (p52). Afterwards hotfoot it to your dinner booking at the Press Club (p47).

DAY TWO

Have coffee at the legendary Pellegrini's Espresso Bar (p49) or the City Wine Shop (p49), then take a stroll around the Royal Exhibition Building (p103). Immerse yourself in the Melbourne Museum (p103), then do a lap of Lygon St and stop in at one of Carlton's cafes for a piadina or pasta lunch. Make your way to Fitzroy for some shopping on Brunswick and Gertrude Sts (p91). You'll deserve a pot at a Fitzroy pub by beer o'clock, then catch a gallery opening or tram it back into town for drinks at Riverland (p51) followed by a casual dinner at Bar Lourinhã (p44) or Cumulus Inc (p45). Get your dancing shoes on and head to Miss Libertine (p52).

Top Checking out the cakes on Acland St, St Kilda (p114) **Bottom** Royal Exhibition Building (p103), a shining example of Melbourne's architectural heritage

DAY THREE

Grab a fortifying coffee at Sensory Lab (p49) then wander across the misty Yarra River to Southbank. Take a vertiginous peek at the city from the Eureka Skydeck 88 (p56). Jump on a St Kilda Rd tram and head to St Kilda beach for a walk along the Esplanade. Grab lunch at Café di Stasio (p115), Circa at the Prince (p115) or Mirka at Tolarno (p116), or if the day's too good to miss, eat fish and chips on the pier. Wander back to Acland St for a browse and grab some poppy-seed cake for afternoon tea. Then make a night of it at one of Fitzroy St's bars or catch a band at the Esplanade Hotel (p117) or Richmond's Corner Hotel (p87).

SUMMERTIME SATURDAY

Start the day with a bucolic stroll at a farmers market (www.mfm.com .au). Hire a bike and cycle along the Yarra, or take a cruise. Head to the beach at South Melbourne, then stroll down Albert Park's Victoria Ave and lunch in your thongs (flip flops). If it's hot, local swimming pools are also good to cool off in. Slurp a blood-orange granita from Brunetti (p108) or sip a glass of sparkling at the airy Panama Dining Room (p99) or at the Carlton Hotel's Palmz (p48). Balmy evening? Head to Rooftop Cinema (p160) for the wonderful view of Swanston St's art deco towers, stripy French deckchairs and the postflick bar scene.

FORWARD PLANNING

Three weeks before you go Organise your accommodation (and check the diary on p19 to see if your visit is coinciding with any major events); try to nab a table Vue de Monde (p47) or if pizza is more appealing, make your reservation at Ladro (p99); look out for what appeals at the Victorian Arts Centre (p61), the Malthouse Theatre (p60) or one of Melbourne's many live-music venues, and book your tickets.

One week before you go Read the week's Three Thousand (www.threethousand.com .au) missive, sign up to Michigirl (http://michigirl.com.au) and see what sales Missy Confidential (www.missyconfidential.com.au) has discovered; check Ticketmaster for AFL games; browse the *Age* (www.theage.com.au) for new bar and restaurant openings; check the week's weather and pack accordingly (don't forget the sunblock, even in winter).

One day before you go Make sure you return restaurant confirmation calls; check you've packed a couple of extra pieces of clothing – a scarf and a singlet – in case of unexpected hot or cold snaps; stock up on vitamin B for stamina.

Collingwood Children's Farm (p101), Abbotsford, enjoyed by kids of all species

TRENT PATON

KIDS

The Melbourne Aquarium (p39) lets kids walk among the fish, and the Melbourne Museum (p103) has a dedicated kids' area (or play pirates on the Polly Woodside (p60). ArtPlay in Birrarung Marr (p38) has inspiring weekend and holiday workshops, though you'll need to book ahead. Or head to the Ian Potter Foundation Children's Garden (p79) in the Royal Botanic Gardens for some environmental adventure. The indoor wave pool and water slides make the Melbourne Sports & Aquatic Centre (p69) a good all-weather option. Put together a picnic at the Queen Victoria Market (p40) and take the punt to Herring Island (p71), or let the kids run free with their barnyard friends at the Collingwood Children's Farm (p101).

>NEIGHBOURHOODS

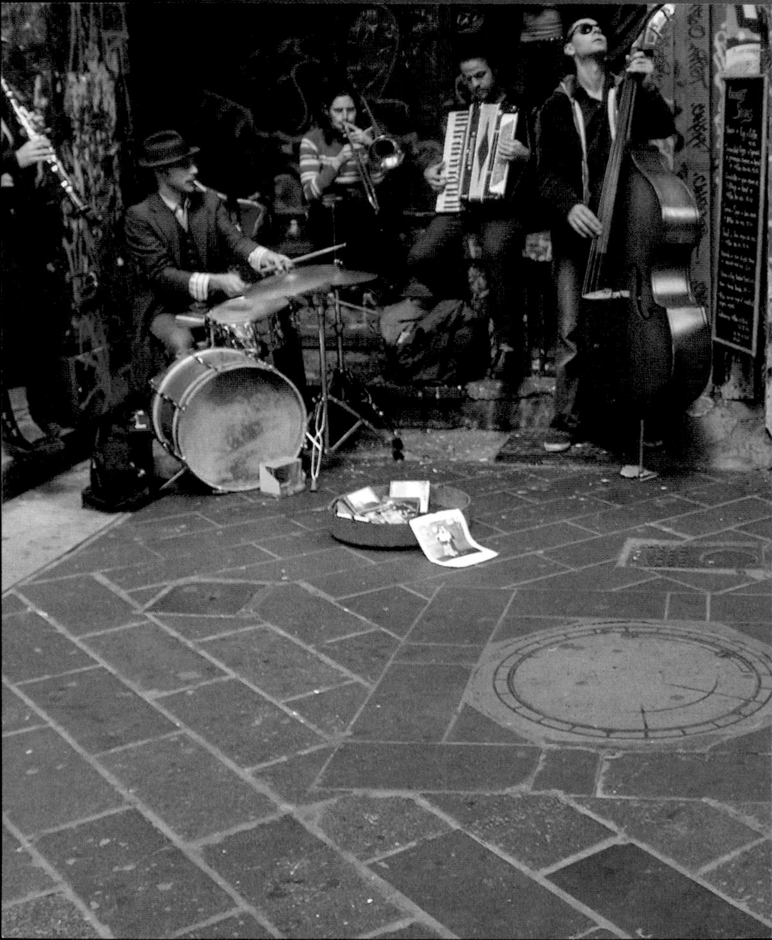

PHIL WEYMOUTH / LONELY PLANET IMAGES
Jazz band playing in Centre Place, city centre

NEIGHBOURHOODS

Melbourne is split in two by the turbid, winding Yarra River. This divide was once more than a physical one, but blanket gentrification of inner-city neighbourhoods has made north–south class and lifestyle distinctions moot, if not entirely indiscernible.

Melbourne's city centre lies just to the north of the river. Locals do bang on about 'the grid', and the city is indeed a strict matrix of ramrod-straight streets, oriented at an angle to the Yarra. The city is used by a broad sweep of citizens to work, shop and socialise. Bars may get suity weekdays after work, but there's an ever-changing mix of moods, crowds and venues.

Docklands sits to the city centre's west, beyond the flowing-roofed Southern Cross Station and Docklands Stadium. On Docklands' far side are a series of still-working docks and the western suburbs. To the east, beyond Fitzroy Gardens, is the sedate residential neighbourhood of East Melbourne, then the outlet strips, Vietnamese restaurants and providores of Richmond.

The inner northern suburbs of Carlton, North Melbourne, Parkville and Brunswick blur out from the city fringe, with a laid-back mix of university buildings, parklands, shops, cafes and restaurants, many within walking distance of the city. On the northeastern side, Fitzroy and Collingwood offer a mix of unique shops and cafes, as well as gently bohemian pubs and bars.

South of the river, Southbank is home to the city's arts big guns (including the sprawling campus of the Victorian College of the Arts). The grand tree-lined boulevard of St Kilda Rd is bedecked with office blocks. Parkland stretches from the Yarra's edge through the Domain, the Royal Botanical Gardens and Fawkner Park to the streets of leafy, upmarket South Yarra and Toorak and their younger, hipper neighbours Prahran and Windsor. Further south, bayside St Kilda is a busy, hedonistic hub. Chi-chi Albert Park, South Melbourne and Port Melbourne share a slice of Port Phillip Bay further to the west.

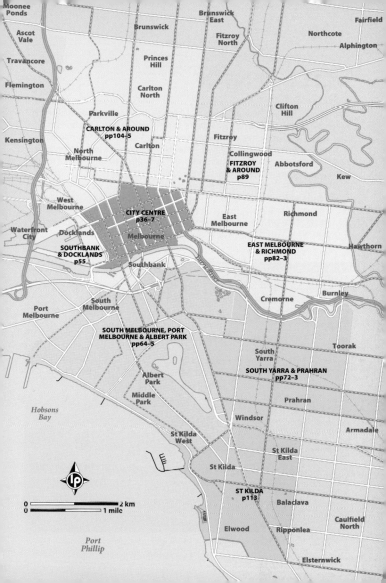

Moonee
Ponds

Ascot
Vale

Brunswick
East

Fairfield

Brunswick

Fitzroy
North

Northcote

Travancore

Alphington

Princes
Hill

Flemington

Carlton
North

Clifton
Hill

Parkville

CARLTON & AROUND
pp104–5

Fitzroy

Kensington

North
Melbourne

Carlton

Collingwood

FITZROY
& AROUND
p89

Abbotsford

Kew

West
Melbourne

CITY CENTRE
p36–7

East
Melbourne

Richmond

Waterfront
City

Docklands

Melbourne

SOUTHBANK
& DOCKLANDS
p55

EAST MELBOURNE
& RICHMOND
pp82–3

Hawthorn

Southbank

Port
Melbourne

South
Melbourne

Cremorne

Burnley

SOUTH MELBOURNE, PORT
MELBOURNE & ALBERT PARK
pp64–5

Toorak

South
Yarra

Albert
Park

SOUTH YARRA & PRAHRAN
pp72–3

Middle
Park

Prahran

Hobsons
Bay

Windsor

Armadale

St Kilda
West

St Kilda
East

St Kilda

ST KILDA
p113

Balaclava

0   2 km
0   1 mile

Elwood

Ripponlea

Caulfield
North

Port
Phillip

Elsternwick

>CITY CENTRE

Melbourne's city centre is unlike any other in Australia. Its wide main streets and legion laneways pop and fizz day and night, seven days a week. While many Melburnians make their home in the suburbs, the city centre has an increasingly large residential population. The buildings at the city's heart remain relatively low-rise, lending the main shopping and entertainment areas a human scale. There are two big ends of town, with skyscrapers clustering on the east and west ends of the city grid. Southern Cross Station sits to the west, with Docklands Stadium and Docklands beyond. Opposite the central Flinders St Station, Federation Sq, universally known as Fed Sq, squats beside the Yarra. Its inscribed Kimberly-stone piazza echoes the town squares of Europe, its building's reptilian skin takes its cue from the lines of the city's own street plan.

The illuminated Flinders St Station

TONY HOOD

CITY CENTRE

◉ SEE

⬛ SHOP

🍴 EAT

🍸 DRINK

⭐ PLAY

Please see over for map

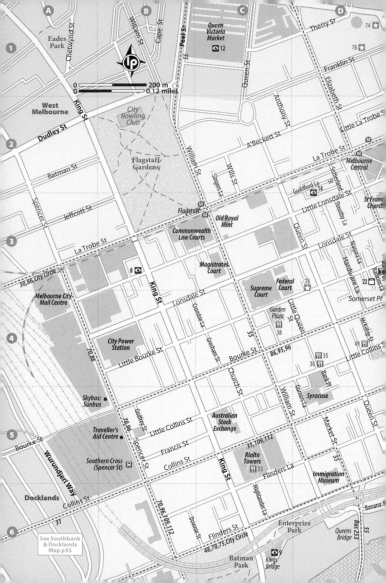

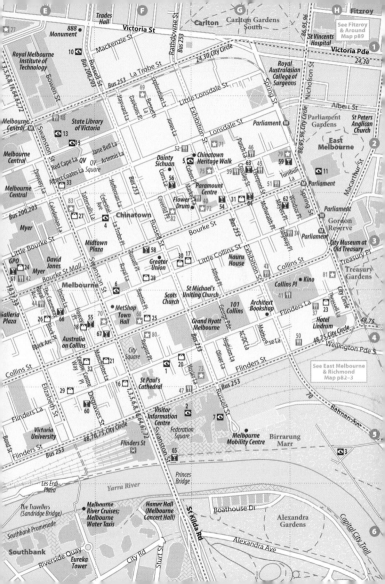

NEIGHBOURHOODS

CITY CENTRE

◉ SEE

◉ ANNA SCHWARTZ GALLERY
☎ 9654 6131; www.annaschwartz gallery.com; 185 Flinders Lane; ☽ noon-6pm Tue-Fri, 1-5pm Sat
Redoubtable Anna Schwartz keeps the city's most respected stable of artists, as well as representing midcareer names from around the country. The gallery is your standard white cube, the work often fiercely conceptual.

◉ AUSTRALIAN CENTRE FOR THE MOVING IMAGE
ACMI; ☎ 8663 2200; www.acmi.net.au; Federation Sq; ☽ 10am-6pm
Innovative ACMI is devoted entirely to screen-based culture and houses a screen gallery and two cinemas. Exhibitions range from the work of Pixar to cutting-edge game and digital designs.

◉ BIRRARUNG MARR
btwn Federation Sq & the Yarra River
Birrarung Marr ('river of mists' in the language of the Wurundjeri people) is the newest addition to Melbourne's parkland fringe,

thoughtfully planned and planted entirely with indigenous flora. The sculptural **Federation Bells** perched on the park's upper level ring out thrice daily with specially commissioned contemporary compositions. An old railway building houses **ArtPlay** (☎ 9664 7900; www .artplay.com.au), which runs creative workshops for children and teens.

◉ CHINATOWN
Little Bourke St, btwn Spring & Swanston Sts
Chinese miners arrived in search of the 'new gold mountain' in the 1850s and settled on this strip of Little Bourke St, now flanked by red archways. Many of the original 19th-century buildings remain, and there's a bustling mix of shops, bars and restaurants, as well as the **Chinese Museum** (☎ 9662 2888; www.chinesemuseum.com.au; 22 Cohen Pl; adult/child $7.50/5.50; ☽ 10am-5pm).

◉ IAN POTTER CENTRE: NGV AUSTRALIA
NGVA; ☎ 8620 2222; www.ngv.vic.gov .au; Federation Sq; admission free; ☽ 10am-5pm Tue-Sun

The companion gallery to the National Gallery of Victoria International (NGVI; p56), this space houses more than 25,000 Australian works. The powerful and challenging indigenous collection, in a dedicated space on the ground floor, is a must-see. See also p12.

◎ KOORIE HERITAGE TRUST
☎ 8622 2600; www.koorieheritagetrust .com; 295 King St; admission by gold coin donation; ◷ 10am-4pm daily

There are gallery spaces, a model scar tree at the centre's heart, changing exhibitions and a shop, as well as a permanent chronological display of Victorian Koorie history that is as moving as it is informative.

◎ MELBOURNE AQUARIUM
☎ 9923 5999; www.melbourne aquarium.com.au; cnr Queenswharf Rd & King St; adult/child/family $33.50/19/89.50; ◷ 9.30am-6pm daily

Rays, gropers and sharks cruise around a 2.2-million-litre tank, watched closely by visitors from a see-through tunnel that traverses the aquarium floor. Kids' activities are run all weekend.

JENNIFER SMITH

Children folk are encouraged to make tracks to Birrarung Marr's ArtPlay creative workshop

---

IT'S EASY BEING GREEN

Melburnians weren't sure what to think about **Council House 2** (CH2; ☎ 9658 9658; 218-242 Little Collins St) during its construction. What looked like being just another grey corporate box has instead turned out to be iridescently, award-winningly green.

Officially opened in August 2006, CH2's design is based on 'biomimicry', reflecting the complex ecosystem of the planet. The building uses the elemental forces of sun, water and wind in combination with a slew of sustainable technologies. These include a basement water-mining plant, a facade of lovely wooden louvres that track the sun (powered by photovoltaic cells), and light and dark air circulation ducts that either absorb heat or draw in fresh air from the roof. The foyer includes an arresting installation by Janet Laurence, evoking the hydrology at work beneath the floor.

CH2 is Melbourne's simple answer to the urgent need to create buildings that are healthier for occupants, financially viable for owners and a lot less hungry for finite resources. All the better for reaching the city council's own targets of zero emissions by 2020.

OLD MELBOURNE GAOL

☎ 8663 7228; www.oldmelbournegaol.com.au; Russell St; adult/child/family $22/12/52, night tour adult/child $35/30; ⏲ 9.30am-5pm

This bleak bluestone monument to 19th-century justice is now a museum. The prison's most famous inmate was bushranger Ned Kelly; his death mask and armour are a prime attraction. For extra frisson, take a **night tour** (☎ 13 28 49; premier.ticketek.com.au) by candlelight.

PARLIAMENT HOUSE

☎ 9651 8911; www.parliament.vic.gov.au; Spring St

This government building's beautiful classical lines and exuberant use of ornamental plasterwork, stencilling and gilt is full of gold rush–era pride and optimism.

Free half-hour **tours** (⏲ 9.30am, 10.30am, 11.30am, 1.30pm, 2.30pm & 3.45pm weekdays) take in the upper and lower houses and the library.

QUEEN VICTORIA MARKET

☎ 9320 5822; www.qvm.com.au; 513 Elizabeth St; ⏲ 6am-2pm Tue & Thu, 6am-5pm Fri, 6am-3pm Sat, 9am-4pm Sun

Melburnians love to shop at the 'Vic'. Fresh produce includes organics and Asian specialities, plus there are deli, meat and fish halls. Clothing and knick-knack stalls dominate on Sundays. While it's big on variety, don't come looking for style.

STATE LIBRARY OF VICTORIA

☎ 8664 7000; www.slv.vic.gov.au; 328 Swanston St; ⏲ 10am-9pm Mon-Thu, 10am-6pm Fri-Sun

Join the bibliophiles and students in quiet contemplation of the magnificent domed La Trobe Reading Room. The library has regular exhibitions of its rare and unusual treasures, and a fine collection of 20th-century portraiture focussing on artists and authors. Bookworm-chic cafe, **Mr Tulk** (☎ 8660 5700; cnr La Trobe & Swanston Sts) serves coffee, wine, meals and treats every day except Sunday.

◎ UTOPIAN SLUMPS
☎ 9077 9918; 33 Guildford Lane;
☼ noon-6pm Wed-Sun
Hidden up gallery-rich Guildford Lane is Utopian Slumps, a curator-run dealer gallery with a stable of some 10 artists. Its glaringly white warehouse space is filled with a changing tapestry of the work of up-and-coming artists.

◎ WHEELER CENTRE
☎ 9094 7800; www.wheelercentre.com;
176 Little Lonsdale St
This new centre (named after Lonely Planet founders Maureen and Tony Wheeler) schedules a range of speakers (usually writers, but also academics and musicians) to talk about all manner of topics. The centre's a celebration of Unesco's acknowledgment of Melbourne as a City of Literature. Free weekly Lunchbox/Soapbox sessions make for a great lunchtime diversion.

▢ SHOP
▢ ALICE EUPHEMIA
Fashion, Accessories
☎ 9650 4300; www.aliceeuphemia.com;
Shop 6, Cathedral Arcade, 37 Swanston St
Art-school cheek abounds in the labels sold here and jewellery similarly sways between the shocking and exquisitely pretty.

▢ BISON *Homewares*
☎ 9650 1938; www.bisonhome.com;
Shop 9, Howey Pl, 273-277 Little Collins St
Canberran Brian Tunks creates beautifully tonal and tactile stoneware that begs everyday use. The shop stocks the full range, including his signature milk bottles, plus some textiles and wooden implements.

▢ CAPTAINS OF INDUSTRY
Fashion
☎ 9670 4405; www.captainsofindustry
.com.au; Level 1, 2 Somerset Pl
Where can a man get a haircut, a bespoke suit and pair of shoes made in the one place? Here. The hard-working folk at spacious and industrial Captains also offer homey breakfasts and thoughtful lunches. To work!

▢ CHRISTINE *Accessories*
☎ 9654 2011; 181 Flinders Lane;
☼ closed Sun
The toile and tartan entrance of Christine Barro's basement hints at

NEIGHBOURHOODS

CITY CENTRE

the bold style within. Art doyennes and architects, Toorak types and club kids meet at this shrine to precious wearables. It's an inspired mix of stalwarts (Sonia Rykiel, Etro, Longchamp) and edgier locals such as jeweller Adrian Lewis.

CLAUDE MAUS *Fashion*
☎ 9654 9844; www.claudemaus.com; **19 Manchester Lane**
Subtly gothic, darkly urban local label by lapsed artist Rob

Maniscalco. Great jeans and lovely leather in a heritage-listed shop with soaring, pressed-metal ceilings and the textured remains of '70s leopard-print wallpaper.

COMEBACK KID *Fashion*
☎ 9670 7076; www.comebackkid.com .au; **Level 1, 8 Rankins Lane;** 🕙 Mon-Sat
Boys with big wallets come here for hip designer threads from the likes of Limedrop. Look for the glitter ball sparkling up the lane.

A bird's-eye view of GPO's fashionable architecture

JENNIFER SMITH

GPO

While buying a stamp in the splendour of the old **GPO** (General Post Office; cnr Bourke & Elizabeth Sts) was very appealing, a post-fire restoration and subsequent reinvention has given Melburnians a whole new post-box of reasons to wander in. The top floor houses fashion heavyweights Akira Isogawa and Belinda. Fashion shoot fave Dinosaur Designs, with its bulky jewellery and homewares, also shares a spot; there's another branch in South Yarra (p74). On the mid- and ground levels are a smattering of Melbourne's most fascinating fashion stores: Gorman, Fat, Alpha60 and Metalicus. After the consumer frenzy, an espresso from Federal Coffee Palace (p49) will keep caffeine levels up.

⬚ COUNTER *Design*
☎ 9650 7775; www.craftvic.org.au; 31 Flinders Lane; 🕓 Mon-Sat

The retail arm of Craft Victoria, Counter showcases the hand-made. Its range of jewellery, textiles, accessories, glass and ceramics bridges the art/craft divide and make wonderful mementos of Melbourne style.

⬚ HUSK *Fashion, Homewares*
☎ 9663 0655; www.husk.com.au; 176 Collins St

Bijou branch of beloved fashion and homewares retailer; for details see p74. There's another branch in Albert Park (p66).

⬚ JASPER JUNIOR
Toys, Children's Wear
☎ 9650 6003; Royal Arcade, Bourke St

This toy emporium also has a branch in Fitzroy; see p92 for details.

⬚ MARAIS *Fashion*
☎ 9639 0314; www.marais.com.au; 1st fl, Royal Arcade, 314 Little Collins St

On a stealthily signposted upper floor of the workaday Royal Arcade, this shop evokes its Parisian namesake with raven-stained parquetry and glossy white panelled walls. International mens- and womenswear labels include fashioned darlings Preen and Lavin.

⬚ METROPOLIS *Books*
☎ 9663 2015; www.metropolisbook shop.com.au; Level 3, Curtin House, 252 Swanston St

Lovely bookish eyrie with a particular focus on art, architecture, fashion and film. It also has some very special kids' books and a desert island discs selection.

⬚ POLYESTER *Music, Books*
☎ 9663 8696; www.polyesterrecords .com; 288 Flinders Lane

The place for CDs, books and tickets for gigs. Also in Fitzroy (p92).

NEIGHBOURHOODS

CITY CENTRE

MENSWEAR

The gentle incline up Little Collins from Swanston St is almost exclusively dedicated to men's fashion. All sartorial persuasions are catered for, from ultra-laid-back Swedish jeans at **Nudie** (☎ 9650 0373; 190 Little Collins St) to the basement of challenging artwear at **Assin** (☎ 9654 0158; www.assin.com.au; 138 Little Collins St), with a gaggle of tailors, shirtmakers and sportswear retailers in between. Have the pros run you up a suit at **Sarti** (☎ 9639 7811; www.sarti.com.au; 144 Little Collins St), then head back over Elizabeth St and try Melbourne's youthful bespoke tailors and shoemakers at Captains of Industry (p41).

◌ SELF PRESERVATION
Jewellery, Accessories
☎ 9650 0523; www.selfpreservation
.com.au; 70 Bourke St
Iron cases hold a range of jewels from local artisans and from long ago, and there is a small gallery space out the back. Not only can you shop for gold and silver, but you can also sit down for a coffee or a glass of wine while you decide on what to take home. Indeed, multitasking never was nicer.

◌ SHAG *Vintage*
☎ 9663 8166; www.shagshop.com.au; Shop 20, Centre Way Arcade, Collins St
Super stylist-ordained vintage pieces, including shoes, furs and bags, plus a great, well-priced collection of fashion-forward Asian-sourced new dresses, jackets and tops. There are also branches in Fitzroy (p94) and in Windsor (p76).

◌ TL WOOD *Fashion*
☎ 9671 4792; www.tlwoodaustralia
.com; 1 Albert Coates Lane, QV
For details of Teresa Liano's designer label store, see p76.

🍴 EAT
🍴 BAR LOURINHÃ *Tapas* $$
☎ 9663 7890; www.barlourinha.com
.au; 37 Little Collins St; ☽ lunch & dinner Mon-Fri; dinner Sat
Matt McConnell's wonderful northern Spanish-Portuguese specialities have the swagger and honesty of an Iberian shepherd but with a cluey, metropolitan touch. There's an intriguing wine list sourced from the region, too. Come Friday night, the sardines are not just on the plate. However, a lone spoonful of the Arabesque *crema* is worth the squeeze.

🍴 CUMULUS INC
Modern Australian $$

www.cumulusinc.com.au; 45 Flinders Lane
Designed by Pascale Gomes-McNabb and co-owned by one of Melbourne's favourite chefs, Andrew McConnell, Cumulus Inc stuns with its casual, ever-changing city space and considered menu; breakfasts include house-cooked sardines with slow-cooked egg, while dinners start with a choice of eight oysters. After opening Cumulus Inc in 2008, award-winning McConnell launched Cutler & Co (p98) and Golden Fields (p120) in St Kilda.

🍴 EARL CANTEEN *Cafe* $
www.earlcanteen.com.au; 500 Bourke St; 🕑 lunch Mon-Sat
This local, free-range-driven cafe is a charmer; take away a lime and palm-sugar-poached (free range) chicken salad, or go the (free range) pork belly. Prices are reasonable and the ethics are great.

🍴 GINGER BOY
Modern Hawker $$

☎ 9662 4200; www.gingerboy.com.au; 27-29 Crossley St; 🕑 lunch & dinner Mon-Fri; dinner Sat
Brave the aggressively trendy surrounds and weekend party scene, as talented Teague Ezard does a fine turn in flash hawker cooking. Flavours pop in dishes such as scallops with green chilli jam, or coconut kingfish with peanut and tamarind dressing. There are two dinner sittings and bookings are required.

🍴 HUTONG DUMPLING BAR
Chinese $

☎ 9650 8128; www.hutong.com.au; 14-16 Market Lane
HuTong's windows face out on famed Flower Drum, and its reputation for divine dumplings and *shao-long* means it's just as hard to get a lunchtime seat. Watch the chefs make the delicate dumplings, then hope they don't watch you making a mess of them (on the table there are step-by-

CHOCOLATE
Melbourne has taken to chocolate with a typical purist zeal. Sample by the block or box, and expect your hot chocolate to be made with couverture. **Koko Black** (☎ 9639 8911; www.kokoblack.com; Royal Arcade) sports a sweet upstairs salon of dollhouse proportions at its original shop in the Royal Arcade (there are branches in the city at Queen Victoria Market and 52 Collins St, and also at 167 Lygon St in Carlton). Sit down for a plate of little chocolate tastes and textures known as a Belgian Spoil.

step instructions for eating them). Also in Prahran (p77).

🍴 KENZAN@GPO *Japanese* $
☎ 9663 7767; 350 Bourke St; 🕑 lunch Mon-Sat

The casual kid sister of posh **Kenzan** (☎ 9654 8933; 56 Flinders Lane) makes the best sushi rolls in Melbourne. Yes, there's spicy tuna, but it also ups the ante with soft-shell crab, intriguing sesame-coated inside-outies, and a range of inari. All come prewrapped for lasting crunch. There are sashimi, *rāmen* (noodles), lunch sets and tea, too.

🍴 LAKSA ME *Malaysian* $
☎ 9639 9885; www.laksame.com; Shop 1, 16 Liverpool St; 🕑 lunch & dinner Mon-Fri, dinner Sat & Sun

One of the city's more eccentric (and, we suspect, ironic) interiors is home to some great Malaysian grub. Laksa is king here, but

there are also some out-of-the-ordinary entrée options like Chinese pastry triangles of diakon, yam bean and chive. There's a nice little beer list; wine drinkers will need to BYO.

🍴 LONGRAIN *Thai* $$$
☎ 9671 3151; www.longrain.com; 44 Little Bourke St; 🕑 lunch Fri, dinner daily

Expect to wait up to two hours (sip a drink and relax, they suggest) before sampling Longrain's fusion-style Thai. The communal tables don't exactly work for a romantic date but they're great for checking out everyone else's meals. Vegetarian options include green curry of tofu and green papaya salad with tamarind and chilli.

🍴 MOVIDA *Spanish* $$
☎ 9663 3038; www.movida.com.au; 1 Hosier Lane; 🕑 lunch & dinner

---

BEER

Let your beer dreams come true (and we're not talking Victoria Bitter) at Melbourne's top beer bars. All have 'awesome beer from knowledgeable staff' according to James Smith of craftypint.com, which keeps beer drinkers informed about the city's brewers and bars.

Head out south to the **Local Taphouse** (www.thelocal.com.au; 184 Carlisle St, St Kilda East), or stay in the centre of things at **Beer DeLuxe** (www.beerdeluxe.com.au; Federation Sq), where staff make time to suggest a good brew. Serving up beer (a lot of it!) is **Biero** (www.biero.com.au; 525 Little Lonsdale St; 🕑 Mon-Sat). See and smell the brewing process out Richmond-way at **Mountain Goat Brewery** (p87; www.goatbeer.com.au; 🕑 Wed & Fri from 5pm).

Movida is nestled in a cobbled laneway emblazoned with one of the world's densest collections of street art; it doesn't get much more Melbourne than this. Line up along the bar, cluster around little window tables or, if you've booked, take a table in the dining area. Movida Next Door (next door!) is the perfect place for a pre-show beer and tapas.

ORIENTAL TEAHOUSE
Chinese, Yum Cha $$
☎ 9600 4230; 378 Little Collins St; ☽ lunch Mon-Sun, dinner Mon-Sat
For details see p78.

PRESS CLUB
Modern Greek $$$
☎ 9677 9677; www.thepressclub.com.au; 72 Flinders St; ☽ lunch Sun-Fri, dinner daily
Melbourne's mod-Greek scene is thriving, and George Calombaris' grand city space gives it the glamour it deserves. There's nothing fussy about the dishes' names (carrot!), but there's a little madness in the detail: *toursi* of heirloom carrot, baby radish, amygdala and seeds. Dessert's souffle boasts single-origin Tanzanian beans, but who can pass up ouzo panna cotta? Bookings are required.

RED PEPPER *Indian* $
www.redpepperindianrestaurant.com; 18 Bourke St
It's mighty rare to get a decent meal for under $10, but it's possible here. The local Indian community knows it's good, and while leather-like seats feign 'upmarket' it's the fresh naan and daal that people come here for. The mango lassis are delicious and you can rock up here any morning until 3am.

SEAMSTRESS
Modern Chinese $$
☎ 9663 6363; www.seamstress.com.au; 113 Lonsdale St; ☽ lunch & dinner Mon-Fri, dinner Sat
Start off with a cocktail under a canopy of tiny cheongsam on the top floor, then make your way downstairs to the dining room for some contemporary Chinese cooking. The food – coconut and roe rice balls, curly fried snapper, Onkaparinga venison with Sichuan pepper and a Chinese wine reduction – is as delicious as it sounds. Its basement bar Sweatshop could be on the cards for a nightcap.

VUE DE MONDE
French, Modern Australian $$$
☎ 9691 3888; www.vuedemonde.com.au; Rialto, 525 Collins St; ☽ lunch & dinner Tue-Fri, dinner Sat
Melbourne's favoured spot for special-occasion dining has finally

47

NEIGHBOURHOODS

CITY CENTRE

KYLIE MCLAUGHLIN / LONELY PLANET IMAGES ©
Outdoor tables at City Wine Shop

in a riotous rendition of haute-bourgeois decor. The shopfront **Café Vue** (☎ 9691 3899; 430 Little Collins St; 🕒 7am-4pm Mon-Fri) does astonishingly good-value breakfasts, brunches and lunch boxes (not to mention perfect Five Senses coffee and amazing pastries).

🍸 DRINK

🍸 1806 *Cocktail Bar*
www.1806.com.au; 169 Exhibition St
This cocktail bar doesn't pack up its stirrers until 3am most mornings (and until 5am on Friday and Saturday). Serves up a long, long list of cocktails.

🍸 BERLIN BAR *Bar*
☎ 9639 3396; www.berlinbar.com.au; 16 Corrs Lane; 🕒 7pm-midnight Tue, 5pm-midnight Wed, 5pm-1am Thu, 4pm-3am Fri, 7pm-3am Sat
And why not create a bar that goes from one extreme to another in just a short walk? Plenty of German beers in your choice of the grungy East section or the fancy-dancy West, though cocktails (try a Checkpoint Charlie) cost the same.

🍸 CARLTON HOTEL *Bar*
☎ 9663 3246; 193 Bourke St; 🕒 4pm-late
Once upon a time, you went to the Carlton because there was

got the views it deserves – some 55 levels up in the Rialto. This is degustation dining with a capital D: you choose how much gastronomic immersion you're up for and courses will be tailored accordingly. Book ahead. If you're after something a little less rigorous, **Bistro Vue** (☎ 9691 3838; 430 Little Collins St) does brilliant French staples (goose-fat frites anyone?)

nowhere else to go. These days, you can still prop up the bar but you'll be drinking a Peninsula Pinot Gris. OTT Melbourne rococo gets another workout here and never fails to raise a smile. Check the rooftop Palmz if you're looking for some Miami-flavoured vice.

☑ CITY WINE SHOP
Wine Bar
☎ 9654 6657; www.citywineshop.net.au; 159 Spring St; ☽ 7am-late Mon-Fri, 9am-late Sat & Sun

The City Wine Shop lets you take home or sample *du jour* drops by the glass from the wall of local and international wines. Snack meals, such as crab cakes or goat's cheese omelette (the bar shares a kitchen with the European restaurant next door) demand you make a night of it. Then you can take the stairs to the all-night **Supper Club** (☎ 9654 6300) and its rooftop bar Siglo.

☑ MEYERS PLACE *Bar*
☎ 9650 8609; 20 Meyers Pl; ☽ 4pm-late Mon-Sat

COFFEE RUN

Melburnians get anxious when there isn't a Gaggia hissing away every 20m, so you'll never be short of options. Here are our city favourites, just in case:

Brother Baba Budan (☎ 9606 0449; 359 Little Bourke St) Cute city outpost of fine roasters St Ali (p68).

Café Vue (☎ 9691 3899; 430 Little Collins St; ☽ 7am-4pm Mon-Fri) Excellent Five Senses coffee and a wondrous range of cakes, pastries and sandwiches. Join the cult that's sprung up around the pistachio cupcakes. See also opposite.

Sensory Lab (David Jones, 297 Little Collins St) Coffee six ways anyone? Bursting out of the David Jones department store is this little cafe serving coffee all the modern ways (those David Jones ladies won't know themselves).

Degraves (☎ 9654 1245; Degraves St) Longtime latte champs keep it calm during the rush; chase a short black with a Bloody Mary if it's one of those mornings/early afternoons.

Federal Coffee Palace (☎ 9662 2224; GPO, Elizabeth St) Atmosphere in spades, with tables beneath the colonnades of the GPO.

Bar Americano (20 Pesgrave Pl) Coffee in the morning and European-style drinking in the evening from the makers of Richmond bar Der Raum (p86).

Pellegrini's Espresso Bar (☎ 9662 1885; 66 Bourke St) The coffee-in-a-tumbler fascination began here for most Melburnians aged over 40. Still serving it strong and with love.

Switchboard (Manchester Unity Arcade, 220 Collins St) Beneath the Man-U mosaics, there's nanna-style wallpaper, cupcakes and a coffee machine in a cupboard.

James Roberts,
Bootmaker and leatherworker at Captains of Industry (p41)

Is there a particular Melbourne look for men? Black, some colour and vintage. **Where do you go for vintage?** I get out of town; first to Brunswick, then Collingwood and Fitzroy. Brotherhood of St Laurence on the corner of Brunswick Rd and Lygon St is good; no cheesy music. I also like Circa Vintage Clothing (p16) for high quality vintage. **Fave spot for dinner?** I haven't eaten there yet, but Vue de Monde (p49). [Roberts was busy making kangaroo-leather menus and tabletops for Vue de Monde at the time of writing.] **If we got to walk a mile in your shoes, where in Melbourne would you take us?** Birrarung Marr by the river, it's a nice walk; Centre Place - I used to work there. There's a nice little community vibe down there, nice people. Then I'd go to Riverland (p51). It's good for a drink down by the river.

Local rock star architects Six Degrees made their mark with this little place, the Ur-laneway bar. Much copy has been devoted to its recycled materials and interesting demarcation of space over the last two decades, but for most Melburnians, it's now just a great place to drink.

☑ NEW GOLD MOUNTAIN *Bar*
☎ 9650 8859; www.newgoldmountain .org; Level 1, 21 Liverpool St; 🕒 6pm-late Mon-Thu & Sat, 5pm-late Fri, 7pm-late Sun

Unsignposted, New Gold Mountain's intense Chinoiserie interior comes as a shock. Two upstairs floors are filled with tiny screen-shielded corners, with decoration so delightfully relentless you feel as if you're trapped in an art-house dream sequence. Sours are the thing, though it does a great vodka sharlotka, too. Harbin heaven.

☑ RIVERLAND *Bar*
☎ 9662 1771; www.riverlandbar.com; Vaults 1-9, Federation Wharf (below Princes Bridge); 🕒 7am-midnight

This bluestone beauty keeps things simple with good wine, beer on tap and bar snacks that hit the mark: charcuterie, cheese and barbecue fare. A rare riverside drinking hole that doesn't have the whiff of corporate investors. Outside tables are a treat when the weather is kind.

☑ SECTION 8 *Bar*
☎ 0430 291 588; www.section8.com .au; 27-29 Tattersalls Lane; 🕒 10am-11pm Sun-Wed, 10am-1am Thu-Sat

The latest in shipping container habitats, come and sink a Mountain Goat brew with the after-work crowd, who make do with packing cases and Chinese lanterns for decor.

⭐ PLAY

⭐ BENNETTS LANE *Jazz Venue*
☎ 9663 2856; www.bennettslane.com; 25 Bennetts Lane; 🕒 8.30pm-late

Bennetts Lane has long been the boiler room of Melbourne jazz. It attracts the cream of local and international talent and an audience that knows when it's time to clap a solo. Tickets from \$15.

⭐ DING DONG LOUNGE
Live Music
☎ 9662 1020; www.dingdonglounge .com.au; 18 Market Lane; 🕒 8pm-late Thu-Sat

Ding Dong Lounge is a great place to see a smaller touring act or catch local bands. Tickets cost between \$15 and \$50, or it's free for a dance after midnight.

⭐ HARDROCK@VERVE
Rock Climbing
☎ 9631 5300; www.hardrock.com.au; 501 Swanston St; entry \$17; 🕒 noon-10pm Mon-Fri, 11am-7pm Sat & Sun

Not the bar franchise but an indoor climbing centre with naturalistic surfaces to 16m and city views. With a few storeys of glass frontage, the city gets to view you, too.

⭐ LA DI DA *Club*
☎ 9670 7680; www.ladidapeople.com; 577 Little Bourke St; ◷ 10am-late Mon-Thu, 10am-5am Fri, 5pm-5am Sat
This large, multilevel space attempts to bring back the glam to seedy old King St. The chesterfield-strewn Public House feeds and waters an after-work crowd; downstairs the club hosts a selection of DJs who spin commercial house or something much more interesting, depending on the night.

⭐ MELBOURNE CITY BATHS
Swimming Pool
☎ 9663 5888; www.melbournecitybaths .com.au; 420 Swanston St; casual swim adult/concession/family $5.50/2.60/12, gym $19.95; ◷ 6am-8pm Fri
The City Baths boast the CBD's largest pool (it's 30m), plus you get to do your laps in a 1903 heritage-listed building. There's also a public spa, the full compliment of gym facilities and squash courts.

⭐ MISS LIBERTINE *Club*
☎ 9663 6855; www.misslibertine .au; 34 Franklin St; ◷ 8am-late Mon-Fri, noon-late Sat, 9pm-late Sun

Rambling old pub mixes its crowd and keeps its musical outlook catholic. The front bar rocks, but the main draw is its diverse line-up of local and touring acts, both live and on the turntables.

⭐ RETREAT ON SPRING *Spa*
☎ 9650 6261; www.retreatonspring .com.au; 49 Spring St; ◷ 9am-6.30 Mon-Tue, 9am-8pm Wed-Fri, 9am-6pm Sat, 9.30am-5pm Sun
Retreat on Spring is an Aveda outfit, so toes a gently New Age line. The relaxing lounge area looks over Treasury Gardens, and the treatment rooms are simple and luxurious.

⭐ ROXANNE PARLOUR
Live Music, Club
☎ 9663 4600; www.roxanneparlour .com.au; Level 3, 2 Coverlid Pl
Music venue from central casting. Up some stairs 'tween porn shop and pool hall, you'll find two rooms of happy indie kids and a varied line-up from rock 'n' roll to electro avant-pop to trance/ psy DJs.

⭐ TOFF IN TOWN *Club, Bar*
☎ 9639 8770; www.thetoffintown .com; Level 2, Curtin House, 252 Swanston St; ◷ 5pm-late Mon-Thu & Sat, 3pm-late Fri, 4pm-late Sun
An atmospheric venue well suited to cabaret that also works for

GRAND OLD DAMES

Melbourne managed to save a number of 19th- and early-20th-century theatres from the wrecking ball. They range in style from elegantly ornate to totally over the top and continue to delight audiences. Curtains are still rising and falling at the following:

Athenaeum (188 Collins St) Dates back to the 1830s and the theatre now hosts Melbourne Opera and the International Comedy Festival.

Capitol Theatre (130 Swanston St) Designed by Walter Burley Griffin and Chicago School in style, it's now an RMIT University lecture hall and used for Melbourne International Film Festival screenings.

Comedy Theatre (240 Exhibition St) A midsized Spanish-style venue from the 1920s, now dedicated to comedy.

Forum Theatre (cnr Russell & Flinders Sts) A Moorish Revival marvel from the 1930s and a venue for touring bands and the Melbourne Film Festival.

Her Majesty's Theatre (199-219 Exhibition St) Red-brick Second Empire on the outside, and 1930s Moderne on the inside, it has been the home of musical comedy since 1880.

Princess Theatre (163 Spring St) A gilded Second Empire beauty that hosts blockbuster musicals.

Regent Theatre (191 Collins St) A rococo picture palace from the 1920s showing musicals and live acts.

intimate gigs by avant-folksters or dance-hall queens. The moody bar next door serves postset drinks of the French-wine and cocktail variety.

>SOUTHBANK & DOCKLANDS

These riverside locales were once gritty industrial areas but they've taken up the hard yakka of leisure. Southbank sits directly across the Yarra from Flinders St. Southgate, the first-cab-off-the-redevelopment-rank, is an airy shopping mall with fabulous views and an eclectic mix of shops, bars and restaurants. Behind here you'll find the city's major arts precinct; the National Gallery of Victoria International, Victorian Arts Centre and various other arts bodies, such as the Australian Ballet. Back down by the river, the promenade stretches to the Crown Casino & Entertainment Complex, where the bread and circuses pull in visitors 24/7. To the city's west lies Docklands. The once working wharves of Victoria Harbour have given birth to a new minicity of apartment buildings and smart offices, restaurant plazas and parkland. It's early days, and its manufactured sameness has yet to be overwritten with the organic cadences and colour of neighbourhood life. But the views are quite something.

SOUTHBANK & DOCKLANDS

◉ SEE
Australian Centre for
 Contemporary Art **1** F3
Eagle **2** D2
Eureka Skydeck 88 ......**3** F2
National Gallery of Victoria
 International **4** F2
Polly Woodside Maritime
 Museum **5** D3

⌂ SHOP
Alexander de Paris **6** E3
DFO **7** C3
Made in Japan **8** F2
NGV Shop **9** F3

⍟ EAT
Atlantic ....(see 10)
Bistro Guillaume **10** D3
Bopha Devi **11** B1
Giuseppe, Arnaldo & Sons
 ....(see 10)
Mecca Bah **12** B1
Nobu ....(see 10)
Rockpool Bar & Grill ...(see 10)

▼ DRINK
Alumbra **13** B1
Eve **14** D3
James Squire
 Brewhouse **15** A1

★ PLAY
Chunky Move **16** F3
Malthouse Theatre **17** F3
Victorian Arts Centre ...**18** F2

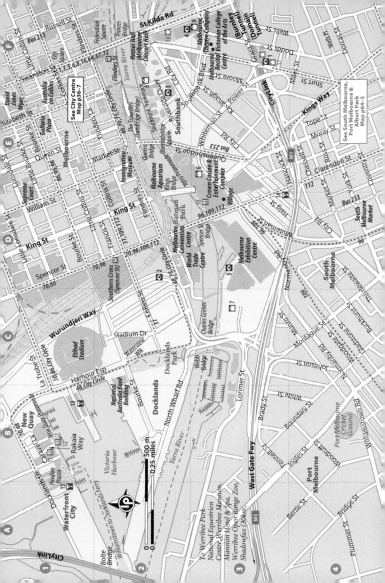

SEE

AUSTRALIAN CENTRE FOR CONTEMPORARY ART

ACCA; ☎ 9697 9999; www.accaonline
.org.au; 111 Sturt St, Southbank;
admission free; ⏱ 10am-5pm Tue-Fri,
11am-6pm Sat & Sun; 🚃 1

This is one of Australia's most
exciting and challenging contemporary galleries. Shows include
work specially commissioned for
the space. The building, with a
rusty exterior evoking the factories that once stood here and a
slick and soaring interior designed
to house often massive artworks,
is fittingly sculptural.

EUREKA SKYDECK 88

☎ 9693 8888; www.eurekaskydeck
.com.au; Riverside Quay, Southbank;
adult/child/family $17.50/10/39.50;
⏱ 10am-10pm (last entry 9.30pm)

A wild elevator ride takes you to
the top of this residential tower
built in 2006: 88 floors in less than
40 seconds. If the vertiginous
views leave you wanting more,
there's 'The Edge' (costs an extra
$12/8/29), not a member of U2,
but a slightly sadistic glass cube
that propels you out of the building; you've got no choice but to
look down.

NATIONAL GALLERY OF VICTORIA INTERNATIONAL

NGVI; ☎ 8620 2222; www.ngv.vic.gov
.au; 180 St Kilda Rd, Southbank; admission free; ⏱ 10am-5pm Wed-Mon

Beyond the water wall you'll find
a collection of international art
that runs from the ancient to the
contemporary. Key works include
a Rembrandt, a Tiepolo and a Bonnard. The decorative arts galleries,
with pieces from the late Middle
Ages to the present day, are
impressive. This is the place where
international blockbuster shows
are hung; crowds for these are
huge and the queues long. The
original building was designed

BUNJIL

As you drive on one of many roads surrounding Docklands (B2), or catch a train to or from
Southern Cross Station (D2), you can't miss **Eagle** (Wurundjeri Way). Let's just say this bird
has presence. Local sculptor Bruce Armstrong was inspired by the figure of Bunjil, the Wurundjeri creator spirit. The cast aluminium bird contentedly rests on a mammoth jarrah perch,
confidently surveying all around with a serene glassy gaze. He's a reminder of the wordless
natural world, scaled to provide a gentle parody of the surrounding cityscape's attempted
domination of the landscape. Upon unveiling, a journalist did have the cheek to call him 'a
bulked-up budgerigar' but most Melburnians see him as the city's true mascot.

Louise Blyton,
Artist and owner of St Luke Artist Colourmen (p94)

Is Melbourne a good city for artists? Every time I return from overseas, I'm amazed how lucky we artists are to work in Melbourne. This city has a great energy and so many opportunities to get your work out there. It's become a hub of creative activity that continues to grow in its own unique way. **Who captures the city's zeitgeist?** Right at the moment I'd have to say it's the stencil artists that rule the laneways. **What do Melbourne artists do best?** Diversity. **What's your favourite painting in the NGV?** Pierre Bonnard's *Siesta – The Artist's Studio* at NGV (opposite): no other painting rejoices in afternoon sex like that does! **How does the city inspire your work?** With so much artistic stimulation you can't help but want to be a part of it. It drives me constantly to push my work further.

by modernist Roy Grounds – don't miss the ceiling of the Great Hall – with a recent interior reno overseen by Mario Bellini.

🛍 SHOP
🛍 ALEXANDRE DE PARIS
Accessories

☎ 9682 1388; Crown Casino & Entertainment Complex, Southbank; ⏰ 10.30am-7pm

Alas, the great Alexandre – the original hairdresser to the stars – is no longer with us, but his lovely range of French-made barrettes, headbands, clips and fascinators live on in this bijou shop.

🛍 DFO *Fashion*

www.dfo.com.au; 20 Convention Centre Place, South Wharf; 🚋 96,112

Head along the Yarra River towards the glossy new Hilton Hotel and you'll spot the bag-carrying army. They've been to Direct Factory Outlets, where plenty of well-known brands offer discount products. Harbour Town, on the other side of Victoria Harbour, is also a famed sale haven.

🛍 MADE IN JAPAN *Homewares*

☎ 9690 9261; www.mij.com.au; Upper Level, Southgate, Southbank

This is a small shopfront of a national Japanese homewares im-porter, and specialises in Kokeshi dolls, kitchenwear and vintage kimonos.

🛍 NGV SHOP *Gallery Shop*

☎ 8620 2243; www.ngv.vic.gov.au; 180 St Kilda Rd, Southbank; ⏰ 10am-5pm Wed-Mon

Although not of the same calibre as the great museum shops of the world, this stylish retail space offers some lovely show-based merchandise, specially mixed CDs, an obligatory range of post-ers, as well as an erudite collection of books.

🍴 EAT
🍴 BOPHA DEVI *Cambodian* $$

☎ 9600 1887; www.bophadevi.com; 27 Rakaia Way, Docklands; ⏰ lunch Thu-Sun, dinner Tue-Sun; 🚋 30, 48

The modern Cambodian food here is a delightful mix of novel and familiar Southeast Asian flavours and textures. Herb-strewn salads, noodles and soups manage to be both fresh and filling.

🍴 MECCA BAH

Middle Eastern $$

☎ 9642 1300; www.meccabah.com; 55a New Quay Promenade, Docklands; ⏰ lunch & dinner; 🚋 30, 48

This opulent hexagon-shaped restaurant serves Turkish pizza and a selection of meze all day. Its mains, mostly tagines and grills,

NEIGHBOURHOODS

SOUTHBANK & DOCKLANDS

CROWNING GLORIES

The Crown Casino & Entertainment Complex, known to most simply as 'Crown', has flashed the cash and lured some star chefs to set up shop along the waterfront. These culinary big guns have come with their own mini-empires and marketing muscle. Local diners are now being tempted over the river to at least try a Rockpool Wagyu burger or a slice of Nobu-ised fish. Here's a run-down of the players:

Bistro Guillaume (☎ 9292 4751) Sydney's famed Frenchman does bistro food with fine-dining flair; the *plat de jour* menu is loaded with French classics.

Atlantic (☎ 9698 8888) Executive chef and partner, Donavan Cooke, has gone fishy at this 'ocean-to-plate' newcomer to Crown.

Giuseppe, Arnaldo & Sons (☎ 9694 7400) Prodigal (and preternaturally talented) Maurice Terzini sold Melbourne's *café e cucina* concept to Sydney, now he's brought Bondi Italian back south.

Nobu (☎ 9696 6566) We're still not sure if Melbourne really needed a Nobu in the first place, but it's a seductive space for those out to impress.

Rockpool Bar & Grill The ubiquitous Sydney chef works his magic; it's a formula but he's on form (see below). Neil Perry has also launched neighbouring Spice Temple (regional Chinese).

are hearty and spicy, and welcome when the wind is whipping up the bay outside.

🍴 ROCKPOOL BAR & GRILL
Modern Australian $$$
☎ 8648 1900; www.rockpoolmelbourne.com; Crown Casino & Entertainment Complex, Southbank; ☙ lunch Sun-Fri, dinner daily

The Melbourne outpost of Neil Perry's empire offers his signature raw seafood bar, but it's really all about beef, from grass-fed to full-blood Wagyu. This darkly masculine space is simple and stylish, as is the menu. Even a side of humble mac 'n' cheese is done with startlingly fab ingredients.

🍸 DRINK

🍸 ALUMBRA *Club*
☎ 8623 9666; www.alumbra.com.au; Shed 9, Central Pier, 161 Harbour Esplanade, Docklands; ☙ 4pm-3am Fri-Sat, 4pm-1am Sun; 🚋 48, City Circle

Beware the meat-market antics on weekends; though it's worth a look for its good music, bar staff and stunning location.

🍸 EVE *Bar*
☎ 9696 7388; www.evebar.com.au; 334 City Rd, Southbank; ☙ Thu-Sat; 🚋 1

Florence Broadhurst wallpapers, a black granite bar and Louis chairs set the tone, which gets lower as the night progresses. Footballers, glamour girls and the odd lost soul come for cocktails and commercial house. Expect to queue after 9pm.

🍺 JAMES SQUIRE BREWHOUSE *Brewery*
☎ 9606 0644; www.jamessquire.net.au; 439 Docklands Dr, Docklands; 🕙 11am-1am; 🚋 30, 48

Big, brassy and boozy. A good place to work off a waterview-aquired thirst. The Pilsner or the India Ale are good for a sweltering day or there are some darker drops for when the weather comes in.

⭐ PLAY

⭐ CHUNKY MOVE *Dance*
☎ 9645 5188; www.chunkymove.com; 111 Sturt St, Southbank; 🚋 1

The state's acclaimed contemporary dance company performs diverse, poppy pieces at its sexy venue behind the Australian Centre for Contemporary Art (ACCA; p56).

⭐ MALTHOUSE THEATRE *Theatre*
☎ 9685 5111; www.malthousetheatre.com.au; 113 Sturt St, Southbank; 🚋 1

The Malthouse Theatre Company is dedicated to developing and promoting contemporary Australian works, so it's worth checking out for some local content. It's housed in an atmospheric old factory – yes, a malt house – and shares a courtyard with ACCA (p56).

⭐ POLLY WOODSIDE MARITIME MUSEUM *Museum*
www.pollywoodside.com.au; Lorimer St E, Southbank; adult/child/family $15/8/42; 🕙 9am-5pm

Polly is not hard to spot; look for the tall ship waiting patiently in what looks like a giant holding pen. This old (1885) coal-hauling tall ship has been hanging around these parts for decades, and now boasts a terrific little interpretive centre, a gorgeous restoration

---

NEW PERFORMANCE SPACES

Fresh love was given to the arts with the 2009 opening of the **Melbourne Recital Centre** (www.melbournerecital.com.au) and **Melbourne Theatre Company** (MTC; www.mtc.com.au) buildings (Map p55, F3). Holding fort on the corner of Southbank Blvd and Sturt St, these award-winning buildings may look like a framed piece of giant honeycomb next to a giant cube, but they are both state-of-the-art performance venues. It's not unusual to see the likes of Geoffrey Rush performing at MTC, while the Melbourne Recital Centre's program ranges from local singer-songwriters and quartets to Babar the Elephant. Meanwhile, on the river's edge, Hamer Hall, the Arts Centre's main concert venue, was due to reopen mid-2012 after extensive redevelopment.

Energetic parkour practitioners act as riverside entertainment, Southbank

PETER LESLIE

and hourly (entertaining) tours on board.

⭐ VICTORIAN ARTS CENTRE
Performing Arts

☎ 9281 8000; www.theartscentre.com
.au; 100 St Kilda Rd; adult/concession/
family $11/8/28; ☾ tours noon-2.30pm
Mon-Sat

Hamer Hall, the circular building closest to the Yarra, features symphonic concerts, choirs and chamber music. (It's currently closed for redevelopment; see p60.) Wearing the spire, the Theatres Building houses the State Theatre, the Playhouse and the George Fairfax Studio, as well as the George Adams Gallery and St Kilda Rd Foyer Gallery. The Famous Spiegeltent (www.spiegeltent .net), one of the last of the great Belgian mirror tents, occupies the forecourt annually between February and April and is the stage for cabaret, music, comedy and circus performances. Across the way in the Kings Domain is the Sidney Myer Music Bowl (Map pp82–3, A4), a summer venue that's seen the likes of Dame Kiri Te Kanawa and hosts dance parties such as Summadayze. The Arts Centre hosts an arts and crafts market every Sunday (from 10am to 4pm).

>SOUTH MELBOURNE, PORT MELBOURNE & ALBERT PARK

Bordered by the sweep of Port Phillip Bay, this string of residential neigh-bourhoods each has its own personality. Streets are quiet and densely packed with single-fronted Victorian and Federation houses. When you do make your way out into the open, it's to a sweeping waterfront punctuated by piers jutting towards the horizon. South Melbourne's pretty streets are home to ad agencies and film-related companies, and its main thoroughfare of Clarendon St is dissected by laid-back but up-market shopping streets, Coventry and Park. Albert Park's Bridport St runs into Victoria, or 'Vic', Ave. Lined with cafes, restaurants and shops, there's a casual weekend bustle. Port Melbourne's regeneration has come more slowly than its leafy neighbours but its cottages and converted factories are now populated with professionals, too. Its shopping strip, Bay St, now rivals Vic Ave for a certain kind of style. The common thread is Canter-bury Rd. It's permanent peak hour on the beachfront footpath along Beaconsfield Pde as joggers, dogwalkers, rollerbladers and cyclists take in the sea air.

SOUTH MELBOURNE, PORT MELBOURNE & ALBERT PARK

◉ SEE
Albert Park Lake 1 G4
See Yup Temple 2 F2

🏠 SHOP
Avenue Bookstore 3 E3
Empire Vintage 4 E3
Husk 5 E3
Izzi & Popo 6 E2
Manon 7 E2
Nest 8 E2
South Melbourne
   Market 9 E2

🍴 EAT
3 Station Pier ....(see 17)
Albert Park Hotel
   Oyster Bar & Grill 10 E3
Mart 130 ....11 G5
Montague Hotel 12 E3
Salford Lads Club 13 B1
Santiago 14 F5
St Ali 15 F1
Tempura Hajime 16 G2
Waterfront 17 B3

🍸 DRINK
Lina's Bistro a Vin 18 E3
London 19 B3
Middle Park Hotel 20 F5

⭐ PLAY
Butterfly Club 21 E2
Melbourne Sports &
   Aquatic Centre 22 F4

Please see over for map

An urban maiden jogging beside the swans at Albert Park Lake

REBECCA SKINNER

SEE

ALBERT PARK LAKE

btwn Queens Rd, Fitzroy St, Canterbury Rd & Albert Rd, Albert Park; 🚋 96

Elegant black swans give their inimitable bottoms-up salute as you circumnavigate the 5km-long perimeter of this manmade lake. Jogging, cycling, walking or frolicking in a playground is the appropriate human equivalent. Albert Park Lake is home to the Australian Formula One Grand Prix (p22), held each March.

SEE YUP TEMPLE

☎ 9699 7388; 76-80 Raglan St, South Melbourne; 🚋 112

Prayers have floated heavenward here since 1866. The high-Victorian architecture incorporates Chinese elements and is embellished with exquisite hand-carved artefacts from Guangzhou. Memorial halls hold the only existing records of the lives of thousands of early Chinese immigrants.

SHOP

AVENUE BOOKSTORE *Books*

☎ 9690 2227; www.avenuebookstore .com.au; 127 Dundas Pl, Albert Park; ☻ 9am-7pm; 🚋 96

Everyone needs a neighbourhood bookshop like this one, which is full of nooks and crannies and

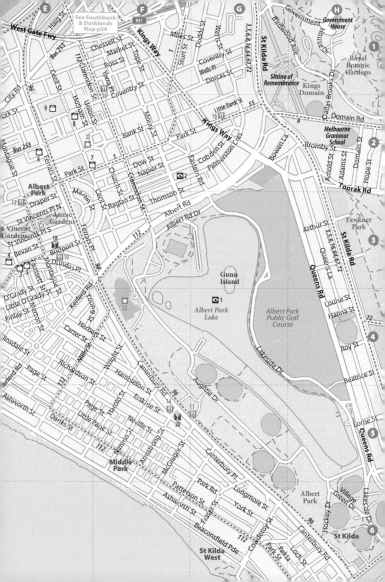

WORTH THE TRIP

Just 20 minutes down the Princes Hwy from the spectacular hump of the West Gate Bridge (off Map p55, A3), among market gardens, abandoned factories and new housing estates, lies **Werribee Mansion** (☎ 9741 6879; www.parkweb.vic.gov.au; K Rd, Werribee; ◷ 10am-5pm). This solid 1870s edifice brims with colonial arriviste ambition and is stuffed with the Victoriana to match. Behind the mansion itself, housed in a beautifully austere old seminary, is the **Mansion Hotel & Spa** (www.lancemore.com .au/mansion), a stylish, modern hotel specialising in peace and quiet. Relax with its clever collection of contemporary art, library, billiards room and large indoor pool. A short, bucolic stumble away is the winery **Shadowfax** (☎ 9731 4420; www.shadowfax.com .au). Tastings and wood-fired pizzas are available in the stunning Wood Marsh–designed space, or pull up an outdoor table overlooking the plantings of shiraz. The Victorian State Rose Gardens is also part of the Mansion complex, and just a few minutes' drive away is the **Werribee Open Range Zoo** (☎ 9731 9600; www.zoo.org.au; adult/child/family $24.80/12.40/58.60; ◷ 9am-5pm, no entry after 3.30pm) and the **Werribee Park National Equestrian Centre** (www.wpnec.com.au).

literary fiction, cooking, gardening, art and children's books. Cluey staff make spot-on recommendations, too.

EMPIRE VINTAGE *Vintage*
☎ 9682 6677; www.empirevintage .com.au; 63 Cardigan Pl, Albert Park; ▣ 96

Lyn Gardener's style is evident in every last piece of stock in this bounteous space. Vintage dresses, aprons, bedspreads, fabrics and jewellery share the shelves with some wonderfully strange industrial paraphernalia.

HUSK *Fashion, Homewares*
☎ 9690 6994; www.husk.com.au; 123 Dundas Pl, Albert Park; ▣ 1, 96

A branch of the fashion and homewares retailer; for details see p74.

IZZI & POPO *Vintage*
☎ 9696 1771; www.izziandpopo .au; 258 Ferrars St, South Melbourne; ◷ closed Tue; ▣ 112

This charming superstuffed antiques shop sources much of its stock from Belgium. There are lots of small suitcase–sized collectibles alongside the furniture.

MANON *Homewares*
☎ 9686 1530; 294 Park St, South Melbourne; ▣ 112

French homewares specialist Manon focuses on pieces with a provincial earthiness and a contemporary twist. The store is a little hike from the action, but all the more special in its corner Victorian shopfront.

⌂ NEST *Homewares*
☎ 9699 8277; www.nesthomewares .com.au; 289 Coventry St, South Melbourne; 🚋 96
This light, bright homewares store champions locals, such as Spacecraft textiles and Aesop skincare. It does its own range of 'comfort wear' that's too nice to hide at home in.

⌂ SOUTH MELBOURNE MARKET *Market*
☎ 9209 6295; www.southmelbourne market.com.au; cnr Coventry & Cecil Sts, South Melbourne; 🕒 8am-4pm Wed, Sat & Sun, 8am-6pm Fri; 🚋 96
This labyrinthine neighbourhood institution sells everything from carpets to zucchini flowers to (reputedly) the city's best dim sims. The fresh produce is excellent, the pace is leisurely and the surrounding streets are conveniently dotted with decent cafes.

🍴 EAT
🍴 ALBERT PARK HOTEL OYSTER BAR & GRILL
Seafood $$
☎ 9690 5459; www.thealbertpark.com .au; Cnr Montague St & Dundas Pl, Albert Park; 🚋 1, 96

With a focus on oysters and seafood as well as bar food, this new incarnation of the Albert Park Hotel (thanks to architects from Six Degrees) is filling seats with its promise of market-priced fish and wood-barbequed 'big fish' served in five different Mediterranean styles. Its bar is a relaxing place for a brew on a weekend.

🍴 MART 130 *Cafe* $
☎ 9690 8831; 107a Canterbury Rd, Middle Park; 🕒 breakfast & lunch; 🚋 96
Where the light-rail trams now run was once a fully-fledged railroad with a string of Federation-style stations. Mart 130 has painted the walls and floors a smart black and white and serves up corncakes, granola and eggs, with decks overlooking the park. Weekend waits can be long.

🍴 MONTAGUE HOTEL
French $$
☎ 9690 9044; www.montaguehotel .com.au; 355 Park St, South Melbourne; 🕒 lunch & dinner daily; 🚋 96
No architect's wit at work here, just a smart, comfortable and essentially old-fashioned space. The mainly French food, with some northern Asian ideas as well, is cooked with precision and care; it's definitely not just an adjunct to a bottle or two.

🍴 SALFORD LADS CLUB *Cafe* $

☎ 0409 543 911; www.salfordladsclub
.com; 1 Fennel St, Port Melbourne;
🕙 Mon-Sat

This former car garage in an industrial area has made good and is now a hive for hip folk (not just lads, of course) seeking caffeine, luxe breakfasts and lunches and, come sunny times, shade.

🍴 ST ALI *Cafe* $

☎ 9686 2990; www.stali.com.au; 12-18 Yarra Pl, South Melbourne; 🕙 breakfast & lunch; 🚋 112

This hideaway warehouse space is a lovely jumble of communal tables, nooks and balconies to accommodate any mood. The food is simple and fresh; modern Middle Eastern–style salads and filled pides star. Coffee is carefully sourced, roasted and bagged on-site, and guaranteed to be good.

🍴 SANTIAGO *Spanish* $$

☎ 9696 8884; www.santiagotapas
.com.au; 14 Armstrong St, Middle Park;
🕙 dinner daily, breakfast & lunch Sat & Sun; 🚋 1, 96

Delicious tapas in a luxe, yet kind of grungy, atmosphere. Paella nights

REBECCA SKINNER
Espresso worship in a warehouse, St Ali

(Wednesday and Saturday) are popular, but you can do the usual tasty tapas then, too. Weekend breakfasts are trad Spanish.

🍴 TEMPURA HAJIME

Japanese $$$

☎ 9696 0051; www.tempurahajime
.com; 60 Park St, South Melbourne;
🕙 lunch Tue-Fri, dinner Mon-Sat; 🚋 112

PORT VIEWS

Station Pier (Map pp64-5, B4) holds many memories for generations of Victorian immigrants and it's still a working passenger port today. The *Spirit of Tasmania* ferry berths here, as do cruise and navy ships. There's a clutch of swish mega-restaurants on the pier itself – **Waterfront**, **3 Station Pier** – serving up bay vistas and variable food to large numbers of visitors.

V

NEIGHBOURHOODS

SOUTH MELBOURNE, PORT MELBOURNE & ALBERT PARK

Completely unmarked door, tiny (seating 12) and almost impossible to get a booking? Cult status is assured and, in this case, warranted. Hajime takes you on an edible journey with a set menu of beautifully pondered and prepared small dishes made with seasonal produce.

▼ DRINK
▼ LINA'S BISTRO A VIN
Wine Bar
☎ 9645 5515; 114 Bridport St, Albert Park; 🕒 4pm-late Mon-Fri, 3pm-late Sat & Sun; 🚃 96

Although serving up admirable bistro fare, this Parisian-styled wine bar is loved by locals as a drinking spot, especially the cheery back courtyard. The *vin* selection is comprehensive.

▼ LONDON *Pub*
☎ 9646 4644; www.thelondon.com.au; 92 Beach St, Port Melbourne; 🚃 109

Once a sailor's first (and only) point of call, today this portside pub is as well known for its food as the coldness of its beer. It's ideal for watching the sunset or the *Spirit of Tasmania* depart.

▼ MIDDLE PARK HOTEL *Pub*
☎ 9690 1958; www.middleparkhotel .com.au; 102 Canterbury Road, Middle Park; 🚃 1, 96

A name change and Six Degrees renovation has boosted the hip vibe of this corner pub. It's split in half – one side for drinkers, one side for diners, and upstairs are some of the city's most fun hotel rooms.

⭐ PLAY
✪ BUTTERFLY CLUB *Cabaret*
☎ 9690 2000; www.thebutterflyclub .com; 204 Bank St, South Melbourne; 🕒 5pm-late Tue-Sun; 🚃 112

This little old house, which is crammed with an extraordinary amount of kitsch, remains a mystery to some. Those who appreciate its eccentric charm go for cocktails and nightly shows of hard-to-pigeonhole cabaret and theatre.

✪ MELBOURNE SPORTS & AQUATIC CENTRE
Swimming Pool
☎ 9926 1555; www.msac.com.au; Albert Rd, Albert Park; adult/concession/ family $7/5/18.50; 🕒 daily year-round; 🚃 96

In the parklands of Albert Park, this aquatic centre features a 50m outdoor pool that was added for the 2006 Commonwealth Games, plus a 25m lap pool, kid-munching wave pool and scream-inducing water slide.

>SOUTH YARRA & PRAHRAN

This neighbourhood has always been synonymous with glitz and glamour; it might be south of the Yarra but it's commonly referred to as the 'right' side of the river. Access to South Yarra was by boat or punt – hence Punt Rd – before Princes Bridge was built in 1850. Its elevated aspect and large allotments were always considered prestigious. Chapel St's South Yarra strip still parades itself as a must-visit fashion destination, but has seen better days; it's been taken over by chain stores, tacky bars and, come sunset, doof-doof cars. Over Commercial Rd and into Prahran, things have stayed way more interesting. They then get decidedly rock 'n' roll as the street winds south through Windsor. Hawksburn Village up the hill and High St, Armadale, make for stylish shopping sorties. Cute Greville St runs off Chapel, and has a smattering of nightlife, eating and shopping ops, too. Commercial Rd is Melbourne's pumping pink zone as well as being the home of the Prahran Market, where the locals shop for fruit, veg and upmarket deli delights.

SOUTH YARRA & PRAHRAN

Please see over for map

⊙ SEE
⊙ COMO HOUSE
☎ 9827 2500; www.comohouse
.com.au; cnr Williams Rd & Lechlade
Ave, South Yarra; adult/child/family
$12/6.50/30; ☽ 10am-4pm; 🚊 South
Yarra, 🚌 8

The grand colonial residence of
Como House, overlooking the
Yarra, dates from 1840 and
has undergone several grand
renovations over the years. The
period furnishing, which once be-
longed to the resident Armytage
family, can seem more hysterical
than stately. But the restored
19th-century landscaping Is magnificent. Tours are conducted half-
hourly from 10.30am to 3.30pm.

⊙ HERRING ISLAND
http://home.vicnet.net.au/~herring;
South Yarra; 🚊 South Yarra

Once an unloved dumping ground
for silt, Herring Island is now a
prelapsarian garden that seeks
to preserve the original trees,
shrubs and grasses of the Yarra
River and provide a home for indigenous animals. Hidden within
is an impressive collection of environmental sculpture, including
work by Brit Andy Goldsworthy
and local Julie Collins. Herring
Island can only be reached by
boat: there's a Parks Victoria punt
(☎ 13 19 63; return $2; ☽ 11am-5pm Sat
& Sun Nov-May) that operates from

Como Landing on Alexandra Ave
in South Yarra.

⊙ ROYAL BOTANIC GARDENS
☎ 9252 2300; www.rbg.vic.gov.au;
btwn Alexandra Ave, Anderson St &
Birdwood Ave, South Yarra; admission
free; ☽ 7.30am-sunset daily; 🚌 8

Sprawling beside the Yarra River
are Melbourne's most beautifully designed gardens. There are
extensive mini-ecosystems (cacti
and succulents, a herb garden and
an Australian rainforest) that are
set amid the vast lawns. Bird life is
abundant. The visitor centre (☎ 9252
2429; ☽ 9am-5pm Mon-Fri, 9.30am-5pm
Sat & Sun) is at the Observatory
Gate, Birdwood Ave. There is also
a special garden for children
(see the Ian Potter Foundation
Children's Garden, p79). There's
also a popular running track, the
Tan which circles the perimeter
of the gardens; see p79 for more
information.

⊙ TRISTIAN KOENIG
☎ 9827 8485; http://tristiankoenig.com
.au/; Level 1, 18 Ellis St, South Yarra;
☽ noon-6pm Wed-Sat; 🚌 8

Climb upstairs to find the
unsignposted space where
'gallerist' Tristian Koenig shows
the work of local and international
artists (through both solo shows
and collaborations). Keep an eye
on Ellis St; it's becoming a hub for
contemporary art.

E Barkly Gardens · **Richmond** · **F** · **Burnley** · **G** · Burnley Golf Course · **H**

See East Melbourne & Richmond Map p82–3

M1 **CityLink (Monash Fwy)**

Yarra River

Herring Island

St Georges Rd

Alexandra Ave

Como Landing

Heyington

Como Park

Toorak

Verdant Ave

Williams Rd North

Rockley Rd

Kensington Rd

Como Ave

Lechlade Ave

Bruce St

Washington St

Grange Rd

Orrong Rd

Lansell Rd

Heyington Pl

0 — 500 m
0 — 0.25 miles

Douglas St

Wallace Ave

Jackson St

Toorak Rd

Toorak Rd

Clendon Rd

Hawksburn Rd

Cassell St

Canterbury Rd

Toorak

Kooyong Rd

Hawksburn

Hawksburn

Luxton Rd

Springfield Ave

Fairbairn Rd

Trawool Rd

Cromwell Rd

Motherwell St

Joy St

Howitt St

McKillop St

May Rd

Lambert Rd

Selborne Rd

Hobson St

Clarke St

Williams Rd

Lorne Rd

Malvern Rd

Malvern Rd

Toorak

72

Mackay St

Murray St

Spring St

Wrights Tce

Pridham St

Bayview St

Aberdeen Rd

Victoria Gardens

Lewisham Rd

Newry St

Armadale

Munro St

Northcote Rd

Kooyong Rd

Moorhouse St

Huntingtower Rd

High St

Prahran

Chomley St

Orrong Rd

High St

Armadale

Armadale

Armadale

WORTH THE TRIP

High St, Armadale (www.highstreetarmadale.com.au): once the place to shop for a chester-field or bid at Sotheby's, picturesque High St's core demographic has recently got a whole lot hipper. Designers such as **Arabella Ramsay** (☎ 9824 4490; http://arabellaramsay.com; 1073 High St; 🚊 6), **Lee Matthews** (☎ 9822 8174; www.leemathews.com.au; 1059 High St; 🚊 6) and **Scanlan & Theodore** (☎ 9824 6444; www.scanlantheodore.com.au; 1061 High St; 🚊 6) have flagship shops here and are joined by other inspired retailers, such as **Chambermaid** (☎ 9576 0529; 1052 High St; 🚊 6) and **Manon Cie** (☎ 9821 0760; 1011 High St; 🚊 6). Dose up on carbs from baker **Phillippa's** (☎ 9576 2020; www.phillippas.com.au; 1030 High St; 🚊 6), whose bread can be found around the city and regions. Even the back streets near the grand Victorian Hawksburn train station boast a maze of shops. Don't miss **Market Imports** (☎ 9500 0764; 19 Morey St; 🚊 Armadale), which lovingly sources its ceramics, textiles and other assorted wares from artisans in Mexico and Italy.

🛍 SHOP

🏠 AK TRADITIONS *Craft*
☎ 9533 7576; www.aktraditions.com; 524 Malvern Rd, Prahan; 🚊 72
Ak's stock of exquisitely soulful dolls, toys and quilts are made in Kyrgyz using handmade wool felt and yarn-dyed cotton. It also stocks a range of organic knits for babies, and for the crafty there are some inspiring kits and materials.

🏠 BIG BY FIONA SCANLAN
Children's Wear
☎ 9827 8002; www.bigbyfiona.com; 617 Malvern Rd, Hawksburn; 🚊 72
The clothes in legendary designer Fiona Scanlan's bright, bold kid's shop manage to be bang on trend, while retaining the whimsy that is the under-eights' due.

🏠 CHAPEL STREET BAZAAR
Collectibles
☎ 9529 1727; 217-223 Chapel St, Prahran; 🚊 Prahran
Calling this a 'permanent under-cover collection of market stalls' won't hint at what's tucked away here. This old arcade is a retro-obsessive riot. It doesn't matter if Italian art glass or Noddy eggcups are your thing, you'll find it here.

🏠 DINOSAUR DESIGNS
Jewellery, Homewares
☎ 9827 2600; www.dinosaurdesigns.com.au; 562 Chapel St, South Yarra; 🚊 South Yarra 🚊 8
Made in Australia chunky jewellery and homewares, also a branch at GPO (p43).

🏠 HUSK *Fashion, Homewares*
☎ 9827 2700; www.husk.com.au; 557 Malvern Rd, Toorak; 🚊 72

Teresa Liano
Fashion designer, TL Wood (p76)

Who do you design for? I design for women who love the feeling of beautiful fabrics and beautifully cut clothes. **Is there a 'Melbourne girl' look?** Women in Melbourne like to be individuals; they will pick up on trends and somehow make them their own. Everybody always says Melbourne women always wear black; it's our biggest seller nationally. **What's your favourite neighbourhood?** I love Chapel St, Prahran and Windsor. It's eclectic: there's the Chapel Street Bazaar, and I love how all the secondhand and op shops are mixed up with luxurious boutiques. It makes for an eclectic mix of people, too, from students to very glamorous women. **Winter or summer?** I love winter clothes and layering up. **Where to for shoes and bags?** The city: Christine (p41), Assin (p44) and Marais (p43) are beautiful stores.

NEIGHBOURHOODS

SOUTH YARRA & PRAHRAN

YUMMY MUMMY ZONE

Just a stone's throw away from the teen-thronged footpaths of Chapel St, Hawksburn Village is firmly family-oriented. Don't slip on the track pants just yet though; it's also one of Melbourne's most style-conscious shopping strips. After picking up a pair of Pomme D'Api first walkers from **Ilko** (☎ 9510 031; 534 Malvern Rd; ☒ Hawksburn, ☒ 72), the Easton Pearson–clad mums make time for the Puglian lunch specialities at **Café Latte** (☎ 9826 5846; 521 Malvern Rd; ☒ Hawksburn, ☒ 72). Then, of course, it's worth checking if Alexander Wang is on sale at **Belinda** (☎ 9510 2287; 584 Malvern Rd; ☒ Hawksburn, ☒ 72). As you can imagine, you can't swing a pedigree cat for hitting a Diptyque candle or pure linen tea towel; much more satisfying than Chapel St if you're after top-notch homewares and finely crafted kids' clothes, or if you just like your labels edgily elegant.

Long time love of the local bobo (bourgeois bohemian) tribes; the clothes on the hangers here are as eclectic and earthy as the surrounds. There's a selection of own-brand teas and homewares, as well as a very good cafe. There are also branches in the city centre (p43) and in Albert Park (p66).

🛍 SHAG *Vintage*
☎ 9510 8817; www.shagshop.com.au; 130 Chapel St, Windsor; ☒ Windsor
Superstyled vintage wear available from this suburban branch; see p44 for details.

🛍 TL WOOD *Fashion*
☎ 9510 6700; www.tlwoodaustralia .com; 216 Chapel St, Prahran; ☒ Prahran
Teresa Liano has styled Melbourne's best dressed behind the scenes for years. Her luscious label gives women what they really want: the loveliest silks and wools,

and cuts that both flatter the female form and subtly demand attention. There's another branch in the city centre (p44).

🍴 EAT

🍴 BORSCH, VODKA & TEARS
Polish $$
☎ 9530 2694; www.borschvodkaandtears .com; 173 Chapel St, Windsor; ☒ breakfast, lunch & dinner; ☒ Prahran, ☒ 6
We would consider this one for the name alone, but it's also the business for spruced-up Polish food and an impressive variety of everyone's favourite white spirit, vodka. *Przekaki* spreads let you sample; the dumplings, herrings and blintzes are top-notch.

🍴 DINO'S DELI
Modern Mediterranean $$
☎ 9521 3466; 34 Chapel St, Windsor; ☒ breakfast, lunch & dinner; ☒ Windsor

The wine list is way longer than the menu (evidence of prior drinking lines the walls), but it's a great spot to dine on Spanish flavours while being looked down on by Parisian dancing girls. It can get very busy.

HUTONG DUMPLING BAR
Chinese $$

☎ 9098 1188; 162 Commercial Rd, Prahran; 🚋 6

In the large belly of the Cullen, an Arts Series hotel, is this younger sister to Hutong Dumpling Bar in the city centre (see p48).

JACQUES REYMOND
Modern Australian $$$

☎ 9525 2178; www.jacquesreymond .com.au; 78 Williams Rd, Prahran; ⏱ lunch Thu-Fri, dinner Tue-Sat; 🚋 6

Housed in a Victorian terrace of ample proportions, Reymond was a local pioneer of degustation dining and still encourages you to eat this way (there's a much-lauded vegetarian version). Expect a French-influenced, Asian-accented

A vodka bar by any other name, the ambient Borsch, Vodka & Tears   MICHAEL RUFF

menu with lovely details, such as house-churned butter. This is mod Oz at its best.

🍴 LADRO *Pizza* $$
☎ 9510 2233; www.ladro.com.au; 162 Greville St, Prahran; lunch Fri-Sun, dinner daily; 🚇 Prahran
A southeast outpost of the Gertrude St, Fitzroy original (p99).

🍴 LUCKY COQ *Pizza* $
www.luckycoq.com.au; 179 Chapel St, Windsor; 🚊 6, 78, 79
Bargain pizzas and plenty of late-night DJ action make this a good start to a Chapel St eve. Reports of suit-wearers being denied entry may excite some.

🍴 MAMA GANOUSH
Middle Eastern $$
☎ 9521 4141; www.mamaganoush .com; 56 Chapel St, Windsor; 🕑 dinner Mon-Sat; 🚇 Windsor
Mama Ganoush offers Middle Eastern food that remains true to its roots while being modern and new. The space is full of delicate arabesque screens; the *kibbes* (ground lamb and bulgur), tagines and puddings are full of thought, passion and flavour.

🍴 ORIENTAL TEAHOUSE
Chinese, Yum Cha $$
☎ 9826 0168; www.orientalteahouse .com.au; 455 Chapel St, South Yarra; 🕑 lunch & dinner; 🚇 Prahran, 🚊 72

It has ditched the trolley ritual, but David Zhou's intriguing Shang-hainese offerings are just as good à la carte. The bright refit of an old pub is a departure, too. The excel-lent tea shop is worth a concerted browse. There's also a branch in the city centre (p47).

🍴 OUTPOST CAFE *Cafe* $$
9 Yarra Street, South Yarra; 🚇 South Yarra
Of the St Ali realm (see p68), this mighty busy cafe has two different rooms to dine and converse in. Our pick? The one where you get to watch the food (including items such as shaved Italian black truffle) being prepared.

🍴 THAI FOOD TO GO *Thai* $
☎ 9510 2112; 141 Chapel St, Windsor; 🕑 lunch & dinner; 🚇 Windsor
The happy hipster nonchalance of the staff and décor, plus a nicely buzzing local crew of diners, make up for fairly standard, if fresh and tasty, Thai food. The menu is also fabulously flexible and the salads are a steal. Plus it delivers.

🍸 DRINK
🍸 YELLOW BIRD *Bar*
☎ 9533 8983; 122 Chapel St, Windsor; 🕑 7am-late; 🚇 Windsor, 🚊 6
The Yellow Bird keeps Windsor's cool kids happy with all-day drinks (including an evil coffee, sugar and

beer shot) and wi-fi access. The rock 'n' roll ambience is genuine; it's owned by the drummer from local band Something for Kate.

⭐ PLAY

⭐ AESOP SPA *Spa*
☎ 9866 5250; www.aesop.net.au; 153 Toorak Rd, South Yarra; ⏱ 10am-5pm Tue-Wed & Sat, 10am-3pm Thu-Fri; ⓡ South Yarra, 🚋 8

If you've been using the bathrooms of Melbourne's best restaurants you'll know the citrus tang of their handwash. Take it up a notch here. After you've showered, a facial (and neck cial and arm-cial) will be customised to your skin while you're wrapped up in a mohair blanket.

⭐ IAN POTTER FOUNDATION CHILDREN'S GARDEN *Garden*
☎ 9252 2300; www.rbg.vic.gov.au; Observatory Precinct, Royal Botanic Gardens, Birdwood Ave, South Yarra; ⏱ 10am-4pm Wed-Sun, daily during Victorian school holidays (closed for two months each winter, see website for details); 🚋 8

This whimsical and child-scaled place invites kids and their parents to explore, discover and imagine. The various mini-environments are

THE TAN
'Doing the Tan' is a ritual well-loved by Melburnians, and surprisingly it has nothing to do with the inside of a licensed premises. This 3.8km-long running track, which takes in the outside perimeter of South Yarra's Royal Botanic Gardens (p71), was once for well-shod horses, but now it's one of Melbourne's most scenic places to sweat it out. Athlete Cathy Freeman and numerous AFL stars have tested their mettle on the tan-bark here, but it is also well-frequented by those happy to just shuffle or stroll its length.

often directed by the seasons and many plants have been chosen to delight kids with their intrinsic weirdness or strong colours.

⭐ REVOLVER UPSTAIRS *Club*
☎ 9521 5985; www.revolverupstairs.com.au; 229 Chapel St, Prahran; ⏱ noon-4am Mon-Thu, 24hr Fri-Sun; ⓡ Prahran, 🚋 6

Rowdy Revolver can feel like an enormous version of your own lounge room, but with 54 hours of nonstop music come the weekend, you're probably glad it's not. Live music, interesting DJs and film screenings keep the mixed crowd wide awake.

>EAST MELBOURNE & RICHMOND

Beyond its Wellington St artery, East Melbourne's sedate streets are lined with double-fronted Victorian terraces, Italianate mansions and art deco apartment blocks. Locals here commute to the city by foot, across the Fitzroy Gardens. During the footy season or when a cricket match is being played, the roar of the crowd shatters the calm; you're in lobbing distance of the MCG. Sports fans will become pretty cosy with Yarra Park – Melbourne's main sporting precinct, attracting thousands of adoring fans every year to its many world-class arenas and ovals. A footbridge over the railway line links the MCG with Melbourne and Olympic Parks. Richmond, once a raggle-taggle collection of workers' cottages, is now also rather genteel, although it retains a fair swag of solid, regular pubs and is home to a thriving Vietnamese community along the Victoria St strip. Bridge Rd and Swan St are known for their retail outlet stores; see the shoppers swarm seven days a week. Church St is where fashionable Melbourne comes to buy bathroom fittings, sideboards and sofas.

EAST MELBOURNE & RICHMOND

◎ SEE
Fitzroy Gardens **1** B1
Melbourne Cricket Ground
  (MCG) **2** B3
Melbourne Parks **3** B4
National Sports
  Museum **4** C3

⌂ SHOP
Europa Cellars **5** C2

⁙ EAT
Demitri's Feast **6** E4
Minh Minh **7** E1
Pacific Seafood BBQ
  House **8** E1
Pearl **9** E6
Richmond Hill Cafe &
  Larder **10** D3

▼ DRINK
Der Raum **11** E4
Mountain Goat
  Brewery **12** H2
Public House **13** E5

★ PLAY
AAMI Park **14** B4
Corner Hotel **15** D4
Hisense Arena **16** B4
Melbourne Park **17** B4
Rod Laver Arena **18** B4

Please see over for map

Forget the city hum as you take in the relaxing surroundings of the Fitzroy Gardens

MICHAEL RUFF

🅾 SEE

🅾 FITZROY GARDENS

btwn Wellington Pde, Clarendon, Lansdowne & Albert Sts, East Melbourne; 🚋 **48, 75**

The city drops away suddenly east of Spring St. The sweeping avenues of these Victorian gardens are lined with English elms; there are flowerbeds, oddly endearing fountains (though many are now dry in deference to water restrictions) and gently undulating lawns. **Cooks' Cottage** (B2; ☎ 9419 4677; www.cookscottage.com.au; adult/child/family $4.50/2.20/12; 🕑 9am-5pm) was shipped from Yorkshire, England, in 1934, and has an exhibition about the explorer James Cook's eventful, if controversial, life. There's also a delightful early-20th-century floral **conservatory** (A2; 🕑 9am-5pm).

🅾 MELBOURNE CRICKET GROUND

MCG; ☎ **9657 8888; www.mcg.org.au; Brunton Ave, East Melbourne;** 🚉 **Jolimont,** 🚋 **48, 75**

It's one of the world's great sporting venues, and for many Australians the 'G' is considered hallowed ground. If you want to make a pilgrimage, **tours** (☎ 9657 8879; adult/child/family $20/10/50) take you through the stands, coaches' areas, the MCC (Melbourne Cricket Club) museum – which is a wing of

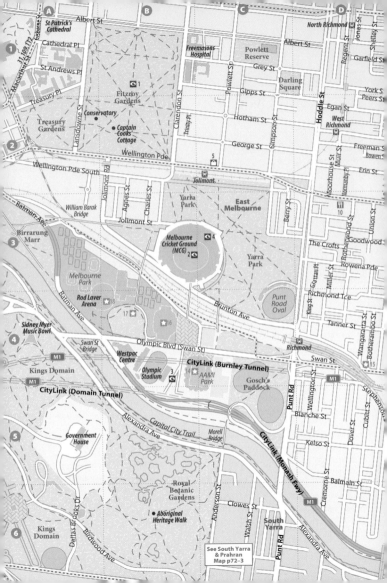

MELBOURNE'S UNIQUE LANDMARKS

You've got to hand it to Melburnians, they have a certain sentimentality towards neon signs and industrial buildings. Things that set off the average Melburnian's nostalgic ticker include the neon Nylex Clock (currently not ticking) atop malt silos near the Yarra River in Richmond (as featured in Paul Kelly's song 'Leaps and Bounds') and the neon Skipping Girl Vinegar sign (renewed and skipping again) near Victoria Gardens shopping centre in Richmond. As you head out of Melbourne via Citylink, you'll spot a favourite silo declaring 'Is Don, Is Good'. (Don's not a local hero – Don's a salami company.)

the National Sports Museum (see below) – and out onto the ground. The tours run every half-hour from 10am to 3pm (on nonmatch days). Tickets for AFL games can be purchased through Ticketmaster (www.ticketmaster.com.au). See also p14.

NATIONAL SPORTS MUSEUM

☎ 9657 8856; www.nsm.org.au; Olympic Stand, Gate 3, MCG, Brunton Ave, East Melbourne; ☺ 10am-5pm; adult/child/family $15/8/45, with MCG tour $30/15/60; ☒ Jolimont, ☒ 48, 75
This new museum features five permanent exhibitions focussing on Australia's favourite sports and historic sporting moments. There's some choice fetish objects on display: hand-written notes outlining the AFL's first rules from 1859, Don Bradman's baggy green cricket cap, olive branches awarded to Australia's first Olympian in 1886, and our Cathy's infamous Sydney Olympics swift suit. For informa-

tion about the Melbourne Cricket Ground itself, see p81.

SHOP

EUROPA CELLARS *Wine*

☎ 9417 7220; www.europacellars.com.au; 150 Wellington Pde, East Melbourne; ☒ Jolimont, ☒ 48, 75
The boys do know their stuff here – they run a weekly schedule of tastings with proselytising zeal. You can often score a bargain on the cellar's European drops, which regularly grace the smartest wine lists 'round town.

EAT

DEMITRI'S FEAST

Greek, Cafe $
www.demitrisfeast.com.au; 141 Swan St, Richmond; ☺ breakfast & lunch Tue-Sun; ☒ 70
Warning: don't even attempt to get a seat here on a weekend; aim for a quiet weekday when you'll have time and space to

Dean Stewart,
Education manager, Koorie Heritage Trust (p39)

Favourite place on the Yarra? The Turning Basin, where the aquarium is. How special and gorgeous that place would have been. **What did Melbourne look like before white settlement?** Colonial blokes talked about what looked like an English landscaped garden: regularly spaced eucalypts, a grassland understorey. The flow of the land is the same; if you don't hold the memory, you're just walking over the top of it. **Where do you find Koorie heritage?** I can do that on Southbank, or in Flagstaff Gardens. I'll hear a magpie-lark and know it's a sound that was the same 10,000 years ago. It's about looking at, and feeling, the place in a different way. **What does the MCG mean to you?** Melbourne Corroboree Ground! Aboriginal people would get together on that spot for gatherings. That cultural connection is still being played out.

fully immerse yourself in lunches including calamari salad with ouzo aioli.

🍴 MINH MINH
Vietnamese, Lao $$

☎ 9427 7891; 94 Victoria St, Richmond; ⏰ lunch & dinner Wed-Sun, dinner Tue; 🚊 109

Mihn Mihn specialises in fiery Lao dishes – the herby green and chilli red beef salad is a favourite – but does all the Vietnamese staples, too. Service is swift and it's always packed.

🍴 PACIFIC SEAFOOD BBQ HOUSE *Chinese* $$

☎ 9427 8225; 240 Victoria St, Richmond; ⏰ lunch & dinner; 🚊 109

Seafood in tanks and script-only menus on coloured craft paper make for an authentic, fast and fabulous dining experience. Tank-fresh fish is done simply, perhaps steamed with ginger and greens, and washed down with Chinese beer. Book, or be ready to queue.

🍴 PEARL *Modern Australian* $$$

☎ 9421 4599; www.pearlrestaurant .com.au; 631-633 Church St, Richmond; ⏰ lunch & dinner; 🚊 South Yarra, 🚊 69

Owner-chef Geoff Lindsay proclaims himself 'a fifth genera-tion Aussie boy who is seduced by ginger, chilli and palm sugar, Turkish delight, chocolate and pomegranate'. We're seduced, too: his exquisitely rendered food really does epitomise modern Australian cooking. The space is slick but comfortable, service is smart, and the bar, which stays open till mid-night, jumps with the fashion-forward crowd from across the river.

🍴 RICHMOND HILL CAFE & LARDER *Mediterranean* $$

☎ 9421 2808; www.rhcl.com.au; 48-50 Bridge Rd, Richmond; ⏰ breakfast & lunch; 🚊 75

A weekend brunch here is worth the queues, not only because you can browse the produce store and rifle the cheese room while you wait. The food is simple, comfort-ing, often surprising, and always made with the best seasonal ingredients.

🍸 DRINK
🍸 DER RAUM *Bar*

☎ 9428 0055; www.derraum.com.au; 438 Church St, Richmond; ⏰ 5pm-1am daily; 🚊 70

The name conjures Fritz Lang and there's definitely something noir-ish about the space and its extreme devotion to hard liquor. It's usually membership only these days; you may need to find yourself a local cocktail lover to help you get in.

⛉ MOUNTAIN GOAT BREWERY
Bar, Brewery

☎ 9428 1180; www.goatbeer.com.au; cnr North & Clark Sts, Richmond; ⏰ from 5pm Wed & Fri; 🚋 48, 75
This beer-producing warehouse opens to the beer-drinking public twice a week, allowing it to enjoy the range of beers (occasionally Fancy Pants, always Hightail and Steam Ale) while nibbling on pizza. Join a Wednesday brewery tour to find out more.

⛉ PUBLIC HOUSE *Bar*
☎ 9421 0187; www.publichouse.com .au; 433-435 Church St, Richmond; ⏰ noon-late; 🚉 Richmond, 🚋 70
Not in any way resembling a pub, this great fitout by architects Six Degrees features their signature blend of found glass and earthy raw and recycled materials. There's imported beer on tap and a short, but sweet, wine list.

⭐ PLAY
⭐ CORNER HOTEL
Live Music, Pub

☎ 9427 9198; www.cornerhotel.com; 57 Swan St, Richmond; 🚉 Richmond, 🚋 70
The band room here is one of Melbourne's most popular midsized venues and has seen plenty of loud and live action over the years. If your ears need a break, there's a friendly front bar and a rooftop with city views.

⭐ MELBOURNE & OLYMPIC PARKS *Sporting Arenas*
☎ 9286 1600; www.mopt.com.au; Batman Ave, East Melbourne; 🚉 Jolimont, 🚋 70
Melbourne Park comprises **Hisense Arena** (B4), with a retractable roof, and **Rod Laver Arena**, home to the Australian Open (p20). The seats and stages at these stadiums can morph to accommodate rock gods and cyclists. Olympic Park includes newly built **AAMI Park**, which hosts soccer (Melbourne Victory), rugby league (Melbourne's league team is Melbourne Storm) and rugby union (Melbourne Rebels) games.

>FITZROY & AROUND

Melbourne's first suburb has had a long history of mixed fortunes. A laid-back, rough-around-the-edges feel persists despite rapid gentrification in the '80s and the ongoing onus of its own cool. Brunswick St, the area's main thoroughfare, sports a straggle of cafes, bars, restaurants and shops that veer between the tacky and the genuinely intriguing, and its back-street pubs have managed to stay a step ahead of the developers. Although most of the artists have moved on in search of cheap studio space, you'll still find a number of galleries and arts-related shops including uberstationer-archivist Zetta Florence (www.zettaflorence.com.au). Gertrude St's rise continues apace; it is flush with decidedly upmarket though passionately individual new businesses. Nearby, the *jolie laide* charms of neighbouring Collingwood's Smith St are also being noticed, particularly by Gen Ys, who come to trawl vintage shops, sip soy lattes or kick back with a beer.

FITZROY & AROUND

SEE
ABBOTSFORD CONVENT
☎ 9415 3600; www.abbotsfordconvent
.com.au; 1 St Heliers St, Abbotsford;
🕙 7.30am-10pm; 🚌 203, 🚊 Victoria
Park

The convent, which dates back to
1861, is spread over nearly seven
hectares of riverside land. The
nuns are long gone – no one is
going to ask you if you've been
to mass lately – and there's now
a rambling collection of creative
studios and community offices.
The **Convent Bakery** (☎ 1300 447
697; www.conventbakery.com) supplies
impromptu picnic provisions or
**Handsome Steve's House of Refresh-
ment** (www.houseofrefreshment.com; 1st fl)
will mix you up a Campari soda.
There's a **Slow Food Market** (www.mfm
.com.au; 🕙 8am-1pm) every fourth
Saturday of the month.

ALCASTON GALLERY
☎ 9418 6444; www.alcastongallery.com
.au; 11 Brunswick St, Fitzroy; 🕙 10am-
6pm Tue-Fri, 11am-5pm Sat; 🚊 112

Set in an imposing boom-style terrace, the Alcaston's focus is on living indigenous artists. The gallery
works directly with communities
and is particularly attentive to cultural sensitivities. There's a space
dedicated to works on paper.

GERTRUDE CONTEMPORARY ART SPACES
☎ 9419 3406; www.gertrude.org
.au; 200 Gertrude St, Fitzroy; 🕙 11am-
5.30pm Tue-Fri,11am-4.30pm Sat; 🚊 86

This nonprofit gallery and studio
complex has been going strong
for over 20 years; many of its
alumni are now famous artists. The
monthly openings are refreshingly
come-as-you-are, with crowds
often spilling onto the street,

WORTH THE TRIP
Up the Eastern Fwy from Fitzroy, the **Heide Museum of Modern Art** (off map,
F1; ☎ 9850 1500; www.heide.com.au; 7 Templestowe Rd, Bulleen; adult/child $12/free;
🕙 10am-5pm Tue-Sun; 🚌 200) is nestled in sprawling grounds by the Yarra. This area
is now deep suburbia, but was once the country home of John and Sunday Reed. The
couple nurtured an artistic community that included Albert Tucker, Sidney Nolan, Arthur
Boyd, Joy Hester, John Perceval and Danila Vassilieff. Heide has an impressive collection of
modern and contemporary Australian art housed in three galleries and scattered throughout the tranquil gardens. Each gallery is unique; Heide I is the heritage-listed Victorian
farmhouse that was the Reed's first home; Heide II, a modernist beauty designed by David
McGlashan in the 1960s, was their second; while Heide III is a purpose-built exhibition
space. Don't miss lunch, or a $15 picnic box, at Heide's Café Vue.

Browsers at the Makers' Market, Abbotsford Convent

KYLIE MCLAUGHLIN / LONELY PLANET IMAGES ©

two-buck wine in hand. The studio open days are worth watching out for.

⬤ SUTTON GALLERY
☎ 9416 0727; www.suttongallery.com.au; 254 Brunswick St, Fitzroy; ⏱ 11am-5pm Tue-Sat; 🚋 112

This gallery is housed in a simple, unassuming warehouse space off Greeves St. It's known for championing challenging new work and represents artists such as Helga Groves, Gordon Bennett and Lindy Lee.

🛍 SHOP

👕 ALPHAVILLE *Fashion*
☎ 9416 4296; www.alpha60.com.au; 179 Brunswick St, Fitzroy; 🚋 112

Alphaville keeps the cool kids of both genders happy with Alpha60's sharp clothes. Particularly delights in architect-black. Also at GPO (p43).

📖 BOOKS FOR COOKS *Books*
☎ 8415 1415; www.booksforcooks.com.au; 233-235 Gertrude St, Fitzroy; 🚋 86

The breadth of this shop's new and secondhand collection is

SPIN

If you find an MP3 download as satisfying as a cup of cold tea, head to Fitzroy, where record stores abound. Try **Northside Records** (☎ 9417 7557; www.northsiderecords.com.au; 236 Gertrude St, Fitzroy; 🚊 86) for DJ eclectic, from Curtis to NY hard salsa to hip-hop; **Title** (☎ 9417 4477; www.titlespace.com; 183 Gertrude St, Fitzroy; 🚊 86) mixes things up with rare-release CDs, as well as arthouse DVDs and music books; while **Polyester** (☎ 9419 5137; www.polyesterrecords.com.au; 387 Brunswick St, Fitzroy; 🚊 112) roams widely but has a heart that belongs to indie. It also has a city branch (p44).

astounding, ranging from obscure gastronomic histories to Ferran Adrià's recipes in *español* to the latest celeb chef's how-to. With books arranged by region, you're in for some delightful, if hunger-inducing, browsing.

🛍 ESS *Fashion*
www.ess-laboratory.com; 114 Gertrude St, Fitzroy; 🚊 86
Japanese designer Hoshika Oshimi and her sound artist collaborative partner, Tatsuyoshi Kawabata, have created waves in Melbourne since Hoshika established Ess Laboratory in 2001. The National Gallery of Victoria has ESS pieces in its gallery; but don't let that stop you claiming one for yourself.

🛍 GORMAN *Fashion*
☎ 9419 5999; www.gorman.ws; 285 Brunswick St, Fitzroy; 🚊 112
Lisa Gorman makes everyday clothes that are far from ordinary: boyish but sexy shapes are cut

from exquisite fabrics, pretty cardies are coupled with relaxed, organic tees. The store is a contemporary fairytale in itself, part Scando forest, part secret attic filled with velvet butterflies and antique furniture. Also in the city centre (p43).

🛍 JASPER JUNIOR
Toys, Children's Wear
☎ 9417 4139; 269 Brunswick St, Fitzroy; 🚊 112
You don't need a wicked witch bearing lollies to lure in the little ones here; this stuffed-to-the-rafters toy emporium offers sweet sustenance for babes and big kids, from well-crafted wood to the odd bit of plastic, but undeniably cute, tat. Local labels Pure Baby and Blink make lovely gifts. There's also a branch in the city centre (p43).

🛍 KLEIN'S *Perfume*
☎ 9416 1221; 313 Brunswick St, Fitzroy; 🚊 112

Jasper Junior is a treasure-trove of children's toys and clothing

MICHAEL RUFF

Just what you need in a neighbourhood apothecary: candles, rare scents and unguents from far and wide. They recommend and wrap with style.

📷 **LEFT** *Fashion*
☎ **9419 9292; 161 Gertrude St, Fitzroy;**
🚋 **86**

Left champions the looks that only a few can pull off, featuring arts-admin darling Yohji Yamamoto and getting into cashmere coats with Damir Doma. It also offers the occasional flash of Japanese leather goods.

⌂ MEET ME AT MIKE'S
Fashion, Craft
☎ 9416 3713; http://meetmeatmikes
.blogspot.com; 63 Brunswick St, Fitzroy;
🚌 112

Mixed assortment of '70s greeting cards share shelf space with quilts and children's clothes lovingly crafted from '50s fabrics. There's also a range of kits and beautiful materials for the Etsy generation.

⌂ ST LUKE ARTIST COLOURMEN *Art Supplies*
☎ 9486 9992; www.stlukeart.com; 32 Smith St, Collingwood; ⏱ closed Sun; 🚌 86

An inspiring art supply shop for both professionals and Sunday painters. St Luke stocks journals, kits and all manner of materials.

⌂ SHAG *Vintage*
☎ 9417 3348; www.shagshop.com.au; 377 Brunswick St, Fitzroy; 🚌 112

Shag offers shoes, furs and bags and other vintage wear. For details, see the branch in the city centre (p44). There's also a branch in Prahran (p76).

⌂ SIGNET BUREAU *Fashion*
☎ 9415 7470; 165 Gertrude St, Fitzroy; ⏱ closed Sun; 🚌 86

This collaboration between shoe designers Preston Zly and Munk makes for thoughtful fashion. It's gallery all the way, eschewing trad shop for creatively hung clothes and shoes.

⌂ SOMEBUDDY LOVES YOU
Fashion
☎ 9415 7066; 193 Smith St, Fitzroy; 🚌 86

Announced by the sneaker-draped power lines on neighbouring Charles St, Buddy does local variations on the global hipster theme: ironic T-shirts, cult-brand jeans, scenster-in-training babywear and kidult toys.

⌂ SPACECRAFT
Homewares, Fashion
www.spacecraftaustralia.com; 255 Gertrude St, Fitzroy; 🚌 86

An excellent place to find a made-in-Melbourne souvenir that won't end up at the back of the cupboard. Textile artist Stewart Russell's botanical and architectural designs adorn everything from stools to socks to single-bed doonas.

⌂ THIRD DRAWER DOWN
Design
www.thirddrawerdown.com; 93 George St, Fitzroy; 🚌 86

This seller-of-great-things makes life beautifully unusual by stocking everything from sesame seed grinders to beer o'clock beach towels and 'come in, we're closed' signs. Crazy items from Kiosk also feature in this 'museum of art souvenirs'.

Pascale Gomes-McNabb
Architect and restaurateur

What do Melbourne restaurants do best? Cheap, interesting and culturally diverse food. **Fine dining or bar snacks?** It's mood dependant: fine dining for a sensuous/luxe occasion, but I also love small bites here and there with a glass of wine at places like Bar Lourinhã (p44) or Añada (p96). **What's Melbourne's greatest architectural asset?** The city grid and the wonderful parks. Thank you, John Hoddle! **Is there a Melbourne interior look?** There are a few: the warm, palimpsest ethos of architects Six Degrees, the retro-Euro interiors, the 'I made it myself' heroism of the cafe scene and then the sophisticated edge of Press Club (p47) and Longrain (p46). **Where do you escape for an afternoon?** Collingwood Children's Farm market (p101) and the Melbourne Museum (p103) with my son. Or a quick look-see on Flinders Lane (Christine, p41; Anna Schwartz Gallery, p38 etc), or on Gertrude St (Gertrude St Enoteca, p99).

VIXEN *Fashion*
☎ 9419 2511; www.vixenaustralia.com;
163 Gertrude St, Fitzroy; 🚃 86
Georgia Chapman's handprinted
silks, velvets and knits are beloved
by Melbourne women for their
grown-up glamour and sensuous,
figure-enhancing cuts. Her cushions
are as covetable as her sarongs.

EAT

AÑADA *Tapas* $$
☎ 9415 6101; www.anada.com.au; 197
Gertrude St, Fitzroy; 🕐 dinner, lunch
Fri-Sun; 🚃 86

Dishes such as mackerel with
orange-blossom and pistachio
are alive with hearty Spanish and
Muslim Mediterranean flavours.
There are big and little plates and
a good selection of Iberian wines.

BABKA BAKERY CAFE
Bakery, Cafe $
☎ 9416 0091; 358 Brunswick St, Fitzroy;
🕐 breakfast & lunch Tue-Sun; 🚃 112
Russian flavours infuse the lovingly
prepared food, and the heady aro-
ma of cinnamon and freshly baked
bread makes just a coffee worth
queuing for. Cakes are notable.

The artisan's deli emporium, Brunswick Street Alimentari   MICHAEL RUFF

ALT-JAPANESE

We're not sure if it constitutes a trend, but the casual Japanese cafes at the south end of Smith St just keep multiplying. **Wabi Sabi Salon** (☎ 9417 6119; 94 Smith St, Collingwood; 🚃 86) started it all and it's been joined by slick **Wood Spoon Kitchen** (☎ 9416 0588; 88 Smith St, Collingwood; 🚃 86), elegant **Cocoro** (☎ 9419 5216; 117 Smith St, Fitzroy; 🚃 86), sweet **Peko Peko** (☎ 9415 9609; 199 Smith St, Fitzroy; 🚃 86) and the trad **Tokushima** (☎ 9486 9933; 70 Smith St, Fitzroy; 🚃 86). In the same style, but serving up bold Korean, is **Goshen** (☎ 9419 6750; 189 Smith St, Fitzroy; 🚃 86).

🍴 BIRDMAN EATING
Cafe $$

www.birdmaneating.com.au; 238 Gertrude St, Fitzroy; 🚃 86
Popular? You bet. This place is named after the infamous 'Birdman Rally' held during Melbourne's Moomba Festival: you'll be glad you don't have to hurl yourself off a bridge to sit pretty on Gertrude St and eat up Welsh rarebit or dip into leek pâté. Like the rally, it's a little mad.

🍴 BRUNSWICK STREET ALIMENTARI *Cafe* $

☎ 9416 2001; 251 Brunswick St, Fitzroy; 🕑 breakfast & lunch; 🚃 112
Part deli, part fuss-free canteen, this cafe stocks artisan bread, smallgoods and cheeses, and also serves up delicious Lebanese pies with labneh, salads, bruschettas, meatball wraps and homemade cakes.

🍴 CAVALLERO
Modern Australian $$

☎ 9417 1377; www.cavallero.com.au; 300 Smith St, Collingwood; 🕑 breakfast, lunch & dinner Tue-Sun; 🚃 86
A super smart, subtle fit-out lets the charm of this grand Victorian shopfront shine. Morning coffee and house-made cookies make way for piadina and pinot gris. There's a seasonal 'kitchen garden' approach to the European-styled food, and the tap pours a rotating selection of microbrewery beers.

🍴 CHARCOAL LANE
Indigenous $$

☎ 9418 3400; www.charcoallane.com .au; 136 Gertrude St, Fitzroy; 🕑 lunch & dinner Tue-Sat; 🚃 86
This training restaurant for Aboriginal and disadvantaged young people is one of the best places to try native flora and fauna; menu items include wallaby tartare and native peppered kangaroo. The sophisticated decor makes a change from the polished concrete look in nearby restaurants.

97

Marios, a Fitzroy institution

MICHAEL RUFF

🍴 COMMONER

Modern Mediterranean $$

☎ 9415 6876; www.thecommoner.com
.au; 122 Johnston St, Fitzroy; 🕐 lunch
Fri, Sat & Sun, dinner Wed-Sun; 🚋 112
If you need to be convinced of this
off-strip restaurant's serious intent,
the house-roasted goat it offers
up come Sunday lunch should
do it. There's a nice, neat wine list
and posh beer to compliment the
Eastern Med–inflected dishes.

🍴 CUTLER & CO

Modern Australian $$$

☎ 9419 4888; www.cutlerandco.com
.au; 55 Gertrude Street, Fitzroy;
🕐 lunch Fri & Sun, dinner Tue-Sun;
🚋 86, 96
Hyped for all the right reasons, this
is another of Andrew McConnell's
restaurants, and though its decor
might be a little over-the-top, its
attentive, informed staff and joy-
inducing meals (suckling pig is a
favourite) quickly made this one of
Melbourne's best.

ᵼᵼᵼ LADRO *Italian* $$
☎ 9415 7575; www.ladro.com.au;
224a Gertrude St, Fitzroy; ⏰ lunch Sun,
dinner daily; 🚊 86

Breathtakingly simple, just-right pizza, pasta and roasts pack in a diverse, if polished, crowd every night. Book ahead: believe us, the Lazio, smeared with an artichoke and anchovy paste and strewn with over the top of mozzarella, is worth getting organised for. Also in Prahran (p78).

ᵼᵼᵼ MARIOS *Cafe* $
☎ 9417 3343; www.marioscafe.com.au;
303 Brunswick St, Fitzroy; ⏰ breakfast,
lunch & dinner; 🚊 112

Mooching at Marios is part of the Melbourne 101 curriculum. Breakfasts are big and served all day, the service is swift and the coffee is old-school strong.

ᵼᵼᵼ OLD KINGDOM *Chinese* $$
☎ 9417 2438; 197 Smith St, Fitzroy;
⏰ lunch Tue-Fri, dinner Tue-Sun; 🚊 86

The queues are here for three things: duck soup, Peking duck, and duck and bean shoots. The owner's one-man show is a bonus, as is the classic no-style decor. Preorder for duck.

ᵼᵼᵼ PANAMA DINING ROOM
Modern European $$
☎ 9417 7663; www.thepanama.com.au;
Level 3, 231 Smith St, Fitzroy; ⏰ dinner
Tue-Sun; 🚊 86

The Franco-Fitzroy pub-grub on offer here is great value and just right over a bottle or two while gawping at the ersatz Manhattan views. The large space also does double duty as a bar, so come early or be prepared for some happy hubbub with your quail cigar and French fries.

ᵼᵼᵼ ROSAMOND *Cafe* $
☎ 9419 2270; rear 191 Smith St, Fitzroy;
⏰ breakfast & lunch; 🚊 86

Rosamond's tiny interior is a warm haven for the local freelance creative crew, who like the daily rations simple but well considered. And that they are: free-range eggs only come scrambled, but with first-rate toast and fresh sides; there's soup, toasties, baguettes, salads and cupcakes too.

🍸 DRINK
🍸 BAR OPEN *Bar*
☎ 9415 9601; www.baropen.com.au; 317
Brunswick St, Fitzroy; ⏰ 3pm-late; 🚊 112

This long-established bar, as the name suggests, is often open when everything else is closed. The bar attracts a relaxed young local crowd ready to kick on. Bands play in the upstairs loft and are almost always free.

🍸 GERTRUDE ST ENOTECA
Wine Bar
☎ 9415 8262; www.gertrudestreet
enoteca.com; 229 Gertrude St, Fitzroy;
⏰ 8am-late Mon-Fri, 9am-late Sat; 🚊 86

WORTH THE TRIP

A sprawling neighbourhood of wooden Federation cottages and big back yards, Northcote's sleepy demeanour shifts once the sun goes down. High St hums to the sound of a thousand Converse One Stars hitting the pavement in search of fun. The **Northcote Social Club** (☎ 9489 3917; 301 High St, Northcote; 🚊 86) is one of Melbourne's best live music venues, with a buzzing front bar any night of the week. Its stage has seen the likes of José González, Deerhoof and Spoon one album out from superstar status. **Joe's Shoe Store** (☎ 9482 7666; 233 High St, Northcote; 🚊 86) will no longer sell you lace-ups but you'll be pleased with its wine list, or find a cosy spot in Wesley Anne's beer garden. **Meine Liebe** (☎ 9482 7001; 231 High St, Northcote; 🚊 86) does crisp, fresh pizzas in an airy old shopfront. During daylight, grab a coffee and a *ruglach* (pastry) at **Palomino** (☎ 9481 0699; 236 High St, Northcote; 🚊 86) and browse the vintage treasures at **Retroactive** (☎ 9489 4566; www.retroactive .net.au; 307 High St, Northcote; 🚊 86); round the day off with a meaty main or a cocktail at the **Estelle** (☎ 9489 4609; www.estellebar-kitchen.com; 243 High St, Northcote; 🚊 86).

The Fitzroyalty regulars don't mind sharing the banquette space and there are tables out back among the wine. The 'list' at this svelte wine bar and bottle shop favours European grapes with erudite advice on same. Bar snacks are sourced from Victoria's top suppliers; you can easily make a meal of them.

🍸 GRACE DARLING *Gastro Pub*
☎ 9416 0055; www.thegracedarling hotel.com.au; 114 Smith St, Collingwood; 🚊 86

Adored by Collingwood football fans, the Grace has been given a bit of spit and polish by some well-known Melbourne foodies, and while the chicken parma remains, it is certainly not how you know it (more a terracotta bake of char-grilled chook, *jamón*, slow-roasted tomato and parmesan).

🍸 LABOUR IN VAIN *Pub*
☎ 9417 5955; www.labourinvain .au; 197a Brunswick St, Fitzroy; 🕓 3pm-late Mon-Wed, 1pm-late Thu-Sun; 🚊 112

Boy's own beer barn with pool tables and lots of boom-era charm. Upstairs there's a deck perfect for Brunswick St perving and imagining the horrors of six o'clock closing.

🍸 LITTLE CREATURES DINING HALL *Beer Hall*
www.littlecreatures.com.au; 222 Brunswick St Fitzroy; 🚊 112

With free wi-fi, community bikes and a daytime kid-friendly groove, this vast drinking hall is the perfect place to meet up with friends, spend up big on pizzas and enjoy a 'spirit-free' drinks list. The focus is on locally made drinks including pear cider, Victorian wines and Australian beer.

🍸 NAKED FOR SATAN *Bar*

www.nakedforsatan.com.au; 285 Brunswick St, Fitzroy; 🕐 daily 11am-late; 🚌 112

Vibrant, loud and reviving an apparent Brunswick St legend (a man nicknamed Satan who would get down and dirty, naked because of the heat, to run an illegal vodka distillery under the shop), this place packs a punch both with its popular *pintxos* ($2 each) and huge range of cleverly named beverages.

🍸 UNION CLUB HOTEL *Pub*

☎ 9417 2926; www.unionclubhotel .com.au; 164 Gore St, Fitzroy; 🕐 3pm-late Mon-Thu, noon-late Fri-Sun; 🚌 86

Every inch a local's local, the Union comes into its own in winter with the fire roaring and the footy on. The dining room serves generous pub favourites and there's a rambling courtyard and footpath tables.

⭐ PLAY

🌟 COLLINGWOOD CHILDREN'S FARM *Farm*

www.farm.org.au; 1 St Heliers St, Abbotsford; adult/child/family $8/4/16; 🕐 9am-5pm; 🚌 203, 🚉 Victoria Park

The inner city melts away at this rustic riverside retreat that's not only loved by children. The appeal of frolicking farm animals is supplemented by a cafe and monthly **farmers market** (🕐 8am-1pm, 2nd Sat of month).

🌟 JAPANESE BATH HOUSE *Bathhouse*

☎ 9419 0268; www.japanesebath house.com; 59 Cromwell St, Collingwood; bath $28, shiatsu from $46; 🕐 11am-10pm Tue-Fri; 11am-8pm Sat & Sun; 🚌 109

Urban as the setting may be, it's as serene as can be inside this authentic *sentō*. Perfect for some communal skinship, a shiatsu and a postsoak sake in the tatami lounge.

🌟 TOTE *Live Music*

☎ 9419 5320; www.thetotehotel .com; 71 Johnston St, cnr Welington St, Collingwood; 🕐 4pm-late Wed-Sun; 🚉 203, 🚌 86

This noisy relic of Melbourne's '80s punk and postpunk scene will steal the heart of anyone who loves sticky carpets and sweaty, guitar-driven tunes. Both local and international acts feature. There's always the promise of a real rock god sighting in the resolutely grungy front bar.

>CARLTON & AROUND

Carlton lost its crazier edge many years ago but still tends towards the liberal and the literary, with the sprawling University of Melbourne, and its large residential colleges, taking up its western edge. Also home to Melbourne's Italian community, you'll see the *tricolori* unfurled come soccer finals and the Grand Prix. Lygon St starts just north of the city and reaches out through leafy North Carlton to booming Brunswick. The southern end of the strip is full of touting trattorias but things get more interesting the closer you get to Elgin St. Delis abound: King & Godfree, the Lygon St Cheese Store and French interloper La Parisienne keep the locals in Ligurian olives and Moscato. Residential North Melbourne lies northwest of Queen Victoria Market; the area's wide streets have recently seen a flurry of new bars and restaurants servicing the area's laid-back locals.

CARLTON & AROUND

Please see over for map

👁 SEE

📷 IAN POTTER MUSEUM OF ART
☎ 8344 5148; www.art-museum
.unimelb.edu.au; Swanston St, btwn
Faraday & Elgin Sts, Carlton; admission
free; 🕑 10am-5pm Tue-Fri, noon-5pm
Sat & Sun; 🚃 6, 8, 72
Set on the edge of the sprawling
University of Melbourne campus,
this museum manages the university's extensive art collection. It's a
thoughtfully designed space and
its exhibition program, from an-
tiquities to the urgently contemporary, is always engaging.

📷 MELBOURNE MUSEUM
☎ 13 11 02; www.museumvictoria
.com.au; 11 Nicholson St, Carlton; adult/
concession $8/free; 🕑 10am-5pm;
🚃 86, 96
This confident postmodern
exhibition space mixes old-style
object displays with themed interactive display areas. The museum's
reach is almost too broad to be
cohesive, but it does provide a
grand sweep of Victoria's natural
and cultural histories. **Bunjilaka**
presents indigenous stories and
history told through objects and
Aboriginal voices. An open-air
forest atrium features Victorian
plants and animals. There's a
hands-on children's area with
weekend activities, as well as the
cinema **Imax** (☎ 9663 5454; www
.imaxmelbourne.com.au).

📷 ROYAL EXHIBITION BUILDING
☎ 9270 5000; www.museumvictoria
.com.au; Nicholson St, Carlton; tours
adult/child $5/3.50; 🚃 86, 96
Built for the International Exhibition in 1880, and winning Unesco
World Heritage status in 2004,
this beautiful Victorian edifice
symbolises the glory days of the
industrial revolution, empire
and 19th-century Melbourne's
economic supremacy. Inside it's
equally impressive, with extensive
decorative paintwork throughout.
Australia's first parliament was held
here in 1901; more than a hundred
years later everything from trade
fairs to dance parties take place
here. Tours are available most days
at 2pm from Melbourne Museum;
call ☎ 13 11 02 to make a booking.

📷 ROYAL MELBOURNE ZOO
☎ 9285 9300; www.zoo.org.au;
Elliott Ave, Parkville; adult/child/family
$24.80/12.40/56.80; 🕑 9am-5pm; 🚃 55
Set in spacious, prettily landscaped gardens, the zoo's enclosures aim to simulate the animals'
natural habitats. Walkways pass
through the enclosures; you can
stroll through the aviary, cross
a bridge over the lions' park or
enter a tropical hothouse full of
fluttering butterflies. There's also a
large collection of native animals
in natural bush settings.

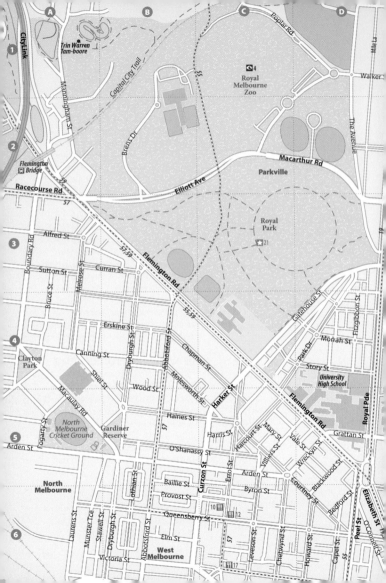

E
F
G
H

To Brunswick
(1.5km)

Royal Pde

MC Labour
Park

Paterson St
Princes
Hill
Arnold St
Carlton St

Richardson St

McIlwraith St

Keele La

Paton St

Lygon St

500 m
0.25 miles

Drummond St
Rathdowne St
Amess St

Canning St

Station St

Reid St

Tapti St

Nicholson St

96

Princes Park Dr

Macpherson St

Fitzroy
North

Princes
Park

Church St

Fenwick St
5

18

Melbourne
General
Cemetery

Carlton
North

Curtain St
Curtain
Square

St Georges Rd

Newry St

Rae St

O'Grady St

Percy St

Cemetery Rd W

Lee St

York St

College Cres

Davis St

Princes St

Alexandra Pde
(Eastern Hwy)

Victoria Pl

Cecil St

Cemetery Rd E
Lytton St

Rathdowne St

Neill St

Canning St

Station St

96

See Fitzroy
& Around
Map p89

Carlton

Kay St

University of
Melbourne

Keppers St

Pitt St

Palmerston St

Kerr St

Swanston St

Spring St

Fitzroy St

122

Tin Alley

Cardigan St

Lygon St

Bus 253

Johnston St

1

19

8
Cinema
Nova

Bus 200,203,205

Elgin St
9
Macarthur
Square

Johnston St
Bus 200,203,205

6

13

Victoria St

Greeves St

Monash Rd

Wilson Ave

Faraday St

Bell St

John St

Kernot Rd

Dorrit St

7

University St

Barkly St

Marchison
Square

Bus 205

Carlton St

Fitzroy

University
Square

1,3,5,6,8,16,64,67,72

16

Carlton
Gardens
North

King William St

Lincoln
Square

Canada La

Bus 240,203

Hanover St

Brunswick St

20

Leicester St

Bouverie St

Argyle
Square

Drummond St

Bus 253

2

Pelham St

Argyle Pl
South

Imax

Palmer St

Swanston St

Cardigan St

Lygon St

3

Queensberry St

Berkeley St

Gertrude St

KEEPING THE RED FLAG FLYING

Melbourne's architectural heritage from the 1870s is all about industrial wealth and empire, but there's one colossal exception. **Trades Hall** (Map pp36-7, E1; 54 Lygon St, cnr Victoria St) was designed by the same architect as the Melbourne Town Hall, and its grand interiors housed a workers' parliament, ballrooms, union offices and education facilities. Unionists still occasionally meet here today, but it sees much more rabid activity in its bar and theatre spaces. It's worth a peek past the International Bookshop to see the delicate 19th-century paintwork that remembers agitators of old. Diagonally opposite, on the city side of Victoria St, the golden orb of the **888 monument** (Map pp36–7, E1) commemorates the struggle for a shorter working day – namely eight hours' work, eight hours' rest, eight hours' recreation – which became standard practice in Victoria by 1860.

SHOP

FILOU *Pastries*

☎ 9347 4029; cnr Lygon & Fenwick Sts, Carlton North; ☼ 7am-6pm Tue-Fri, 7am-5pm Sat, 7am-3pm Sun; 🚋 16

In a dusty, nondescript stretch of Lygon St, opposite the Melbourne Cemetery, Filou's modest counters are stacked with Melbourne's best croissants and French pastries. Its savoury tarts and brioche are perfect picnic-basket fillers, and its bagged biscuits make pretty presents.

KING & GODFREE
Food, Wine

☎ 9347 1619; 293-297 Lygon St, Carlton; ☼ 9am-9pm Mon-Sat, 11am-7pm Sun; 🚌 205, 🚋 16

This cheerful wine shop and deli has been keeping the cellars and pantries of Carlton well stocked for years. The shop has a particularly good range of Victorian wines and also some stellar Italian drops.

The staff here is always happy to help.

LA PARISIENNE *Food*

☎ 9349 1852; 290 Lygon St, Carlton; 🚋 16, 🚌 205

A French interloper on the most Italian of streets, this deli specialises in small goods and take-home dishes that are authentically Gallic. *Boudin blanc* and *noir* (sausages), duck confit and its famous pâtés and terrines will not disappoint. La Parisienne also does a nice range of bread and little pies that are perfect for a picnic basket, and it keeps a range of evocatively packaged pantry items.

READINGS *Books*

☎ 9347 6633; www.readings.com.au; 309 Lygon St, Carlton; ☼ 10am-9pm Sun; 🚌 205, 🚋 16

A potter around this defiantly prospering indie bookshop can occupy an entire afternoon if you're so inclined. There's a dangerously loaded (and good-value) specials table, switched-on staff and everything from Lacan to *Charlie and Lola* on the racks.

🍴 EAT

🍴 ABLA'S *Lebanese* $$

☎ 9347 0006; www.ablas.com.au; 109 Elgin St, Carlton; 🕑 lunch Thu & Fri, dinner Mon-Sat; 🚌 205, 🚃 16

Food and wine specialist King & Godfree has a range that's fit for royalty

MICHAEL RUFF

The kitchen here is steered by Abla Amad, whose authentic, flavour-packed food has inspired a whole generation of local Lebanese chefs. Bring a bottle of your favourite plonk and settle in for a treat Melburnians have been enjoying for over 30 years.

🍴 AUCTION ROOMS *Cafe* $$
☎ 9326 7749; www.auctionroomscafe.com.au; 103-107 Errol St, North Melbourne; 🚋 57
This insanely busy cafe serves up sweet coffee and inventive mains, though sometimes you may wonder if it's still operating as an auction room (everyone just seems so…polished!).

🍴 BRUNETTI *Italian* $
☎ 9347 2801; www.brunetti.com.au; 194-204 Faraday St, Carlton; ☷ breakfast, lunch & dinner; 🚌 205, 🚋 16
Bustling from dawn to midnight, Brunetti is a mini–Roman empire. This cafe is famous for its coffee, granitas and authentic *pasticceria* (pastries). Bain-marie meals can be on the stodgy side (and sometimes that's just what the locals want), but the toasted *tremezzini* (sandwiches) do always please.

🍴 COURTHOUSE HOTEL
Pub Food $$
☎ 9329 5394; www.thecourthouse.net.au; 86 Errol St, North Melbourne; ☷ lunch & dinner Mon-Sat; 🚋 57

This corner pub has managed to retain the comfort and familiarity of a local while taking food, both in its public bar and its more formal dining spaces, very seriously. The European-style dishes are refined and hearty. Lunch deals are great value, and there is a tasting menu at dinner.

🍴 EMBRASSE RESTAURANT
Modern French $$
☎ 9347 3312; www.embrasserestaurant.com.au; 312 Drummond St, Carlton; ☷ lunch Thu-Sun, dinner Wed-Sun
Pressure-cooking chickpeas and daintily serving up emulsions, purees and flowers is Nicolas Poelaert's game, and the crowd is responding enthusiastically. Just off the main Lygon St drag, the space is intimate and formal. Sunday lunch is a four-course ode to France.

🍴 ENOTECA SILENO *Italian* $$
☎ 9389 7070; www.enoteca.com.au; 920 Lygon St, Carlton North; ☷ breakfast, lunch & dinner Tue-Sat; breakfast & lunch Sun; 🚋 16
This groaning enoteca imports some of the city's best quality Italian provisions; you'll see them employed in the menus of regional standards. The Italian wines are also exemplary; you should pick up a bottle and a jar of *carciuga* (artichoke anchovy spread) to take home.

Choosing from the *pastecceria* at Brunetti

KYLIE MCLAUGHLIN / LONELY PLANET IMAGES ©

▥ ESPOSITO AT TOOFEY'S

Seafood, Italian $$$
☎ 9347 9838; www.espositofood.com;
162 Elgin St, Carlton; 🕙 lunch Mon-Fri,
dinner Mon-Sat; 🚋 16

There are no ocean views, modish manners or maritime decoration, just the freshest seafood done with simple Italian style. Esposito only serves sustainable fish and, in the theme of local and seasonal food,

Esposito's mother, Maria, grows much of the restaurant's salad vegetables and herbs herself.

LIBERTINE *French* $$$

☎ 9329 5228; www.libertine dining.com.au; 500 Victoria St, North Melbourne; ☷ lunch & dinner Tue-Sat; 🚊 57

Locals love this small, traditionally decked out shopfront for its real French country cooking. The menu is strong on game, though thoughtful meat-free mains like cauliflower souffle appear between the listings for duck breast and Wagyu steak.

☘ DRINK

☘ GERALD'S BAR *Wine Bar*

☎ 9349 4748; 386 Rathdowne St, Carlton North; ☷ 5-11pm Mon-Sat; 🚊 253

Wine by the glass is democratically selected at Gerald's and it spins some fine vintage vinyl from behind the curved wooden bar. Gerald himself is out the back preparing to feed you whatever he feels like on the day: goat curry, seared calamari, meatballs, trifle.

☘ JIMMY WATSON'S *Wine Bar*

☎ 9347 3985; www.jimmywatsons.com .au; 333 Lygon St, Carlton; ☷ lunch & dinner Mon-Sat; 🚊 16

WORTH THE TRIP

Brunswick (off map, E1) lies just north beyond the expanses of Royal Park. Perpetually clogged Sydney Rd has long been bustling with students and migrant families from southern Europe, the Middle East and more recently Africa. East Brunswick has grown jaggedly into a trendy foodie zone: even cafe's have 'no bloggers' signs on their doors. Tongue-in-cheek this may be, the area is filled with families who moved from small inner-city terraces into larger Brunswick blocks decades ago. Their favourite foods followed them. Stroll into the **A1 Bakery** (☎ 9386 0440; 643-645 Sydney Rd; 🚊 19) for Turkish pizza and baklava, or head over to **Small Block** (☎ 9381 2244; 130 Lygon Street, Brunswick East; 🚊 1, 8) for coffee and cute cupcakes. Hang around for dinner and try for a table at **Rumi** (☎ 9388 8255; 116 Lygon St, Brunswick East; 🚊 1, 8), who gives trad eastern Mediterranean food a contemporary spin. Kick off your shoes in the backyard beer garden of the **Retreat** (☎ 9380 4090; 280 Sydney Rd; 🚊 19) or give your regards to **Atticus Finch** (129 Lygon St, East Brunswick; 🚊 1, 8), where you'll find a judicious wine list. Sit down for some mezze at **Hellenic Republic** (☎ 9381 1222; www.hellenicrepublic.com.au; 434 Lygon St, East Brunswick; 🚊 1, 8) then suss out the band room of the **East Brunswick Club** (☎ 9388 2777; www.eastbrunswick club.com; 280 Lygon Street, East Brunswick; 🚊 1, 8).

Keep it tidy at Watson's wine bar with something nice by the glass, or go a bottle of dry and dry (vermouth and ginger ale) and settle in for the afternoon and evening. If Roy Ground's stunning midcentury building had ears, there'd be a few generations of writers, students and academics in trouble.

ⓨ SEVEN SEEDS *Cafe* $
☎ 9347 8664; www.sevenseeds.com.au; 114 Berkely St, Carlton; 🚊 19, 59
This is the most spacious of the Seven Seeds coffee empire; there's plenty of room to store your bike, sip a splendid coffee beside a growing coffee plant and check out all the other lucky people

who've found this rather out-of-the-way, warehouse-like cafe.

⭐ PLAY
⭐ ROYAL PARK *Park*
btwn Royal Pde & Flemington Rd, Parkville; 🚊 Royal Park
Royal Park's vast open spaces are perfect for a run or power walk and there are sports ovals, netball and hockey stadiums, a golf course and tennis courts. In the northwestern section of the park, **Trin Warren Tam-boore** (A1) is a recently established wetlands area, with boardwalks and interpretive signs for spotting native plants and animals.

>ST KILDA

St Kilda, on the bay directly south of the city, was once the city's favoured 19th-century playground. It's gone in and out of fashion several times since then, and although still affecting the louchness it was known for in the '80s, it has become something of a spoiled brat. That's not to say it's entirely lost its appeal. The halcyon days live on via the grand George Hotel and Palais Theatre. Its palm trees, bay vistas, briny breezes and pink-stained sunsets are heartbreakingly beautiful. Come the weekend, the volume is turned up, the traffic crawls and the street-party atmosphere sets in. Many locals have found respite from the relentless pace in nearby Carlisle St, a traditionally Jewish neighbourhood that's now known for its wine bars, all-day breakfast cafes and quirky shops as much as its kosher bagelries.

ST KILDA

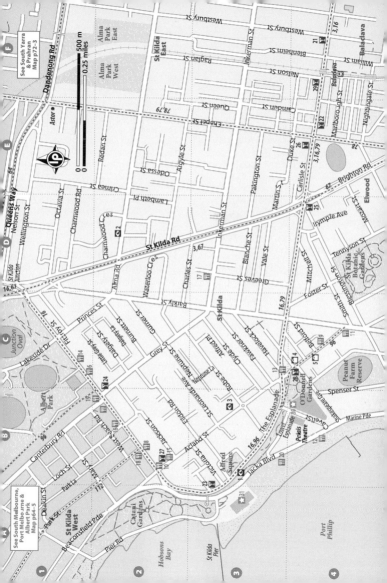

👁 SEE

📷 ESPLANADE MARKET ST KILDA

www.stkildamarket.com; Upper Esplanade, btwn Cavell & Fitzroy Sts; 🕐 10am-5pm Sun; 🚋 96

A kilometre of trestle tables joined end to end carry individually crafted products from toys to organic soaps to large metal sculptures of fishy creatures. Something like 150 stallholders make a weekly appearance; you're bound to find something you like.

📷 JEWISH MUSEUM OF AUSTRALIA

☎ 8534 3600; www.jewishmuseum .com.au; 26 Alma Rd; adult/concession/ family $10/5/20; 🕐 10am-5pm Sun; 🚋 3, 67

Interactive displays tell the history of Australia's Jewish community and permanent exhibitions celebrate the culture's rich cycle of festivals and holy days. The museum also hosts interesting contemporary visual art shows.

📷 LINDEN CENTRE FOR CONTEMPORARY ARTS

☎ 9534 0099; www.lindenarts.org; 26 Acland St; 🕐 1-5pm Mon-Fri, 11am-5pm Sat-Sun; 🚋 96

Housed in an 1870s mansion, Linden champions the work of emerging artists. There's a diverting children's sculpture garden and a peaceful front lawn for postshow lolling. The annual postcard show in February and March is a highlight.

🛍 SHOP

🛍 BROTHERHOOD OF ST LAURENCE *Vintage, Fashion*

82a Acland St, St Kilda; 🚋 96

This op shop sells some of the most retro of the goods donated to welfare organisation Brotherhood of St Laurence. There's a similar branch, Hunter Gatherer (274 Brunswick St, Fitzroy), north of the river.

🛍 MONARCH CAKE SHOP *Food*

☎ 9534 2972; www.monarchcakes.com .au; 103 Acland St; 🕐 7am-10pm; 🚋 96

LITTLE LEAGUE

The St Kilda breakwater is home to a small colony of little penguins (both little in name and little in stature). The penguins, which are of the same species as those on Phillip Island (p123), are not easy to spot and live a rather precarious existence in this ultra-urban enclave. During summer **Port Phillip Eco Centre** (www.ecocentre.com) runs family tours of the St Kilda coastal environment, ending at the penguin colony. It can't guarantee a sighting but will do its best, and all tour proceeds go towards keeping the local penguin outpost flourishing.

St Kilda's Eastern European cake shops have long drawn crowds that come to peer at the sweetly stocked windows. This is a favourite; its kugelhof, plum cake and poppy-seed cheesecake can't be beaten.

🍴 EAT
🍴 BAKER D CHIRICO
Bakery, Cafe $

☎ 9534 3777; 149 Fitzroy St; ⏲ breakfast & lunch Tue-Sun; 🚋 16, 96, 112
The Baker's sourdough is some of the city's finest. Stock up on house-baked granola, or sit down for a coffee, rhubarb Danish or a calzone. Beautifully designed packaging spreads the good taste around.

🍴 CACAO *Bakery, Cafe* $
☎ 8598 9555; www.cacao.com.au; 52 Fitzroy St; ⏲ 7am-7pm; 🚋 16, 96
Set among the trees, Cacao creates award-winning chocolates with the best couverture. It also does a full French patisserie range.

🍴 CAFÉ DI STASIO
Italian $$$

☎ 9525 3999; www.distasio.com.au; 31a Fitzroy St; ⏲ lunch & dinner; 🚋 16, 96, 112
Capricious white-jacketed waiters, a tenebrous Bill Henson photograph and a jazz soundtrack set the mood. The Italian menu has the appropriate drama and grace. Weekly fixed-price lunch menus (two courses and a glass of wine) are great value.

🍴 CICCIOLINA
Modern Mediterranean $$
☎ 9525 3333; www.cicciolinastkilda .com.au; 130 Acland St; ⏲ lunch & dinner; 🚋 16, 96
This warm room of dark wood, subdued lighting and pencil sketches is a St Kilda institution. The inspired mod-Med menu is smart and generous, the service is warm. It doesn't take bookings; eat early or while away your wait in the moody little back bar.

🍴 CIRCA AT THE PRINCE
Modern Australian $$$
☎ 9536 1122; www.circa.com.au; 2 Acland St; ⏲ breakfast & dinner daily, lunch Fri & Sun; 🚋 16, 96, 112
Some of Melbourne's best chefs have cooked here, think Andrew McConnell (now Cutler & Co) and Matt Wilkinson (Pope Joan), and now the baton is in Jake Nicholson's hands. A move – to the Prince's glass-ceilinged courtyard – comes complete with a vertical kitchen garden and promise of food cooked to complement the season. Melbourne's winter is matched with chestnut soup with yabbies.

NEIGHBOURHOODS

ST KILDA

Perched at the bar with refreshments at the Pelican

REBECCA SKINNER

CLAYPOTS *Seafood* $$
213 Barkly St; ⏰ lunch & dinner; 🚃 96
A local favourite, Claypots serves up seafood in its namesake. Get in early to both get a seat and ensure the good stuff is still available, as hot items go fast.

DONOVANS
Modern Mediterranean $$$
☎ 9534 8221; www.donovanshouse.com.au; 40 Jacka Blvd; ⏰ lunch & dinner; 🚃 16, 96
Donovans has a big reputation and a marquee location to match. Overlooking the beach, the interior conjures up a comforting Long Island bolthole. The food is

far from fussy, rather it's solid on flavour and technique, and broad enough to please all comers. Book well ahead.

IL FORNAIO *Italian* $
☎ 9534 2922; www.ilfornaio.net.au; 2 Acland St; 🚃 16, 96, 112
Head chef Philippa Sibley is famed for her desserts, but that's not all you get at Il Fornaio: breakfasts move over for perfect pastas. Still, finish grazing with dessert.

MIRKA AT TOLARNO
International, Italian $$$
☎ 9525 3088; www.mirkatolarnohotel.com; 42 Fitzroy St; ⏰ breakfast, lunch & dinner; 🚃 16, 96, 112

The dark dining room has a history (it's been delighting diners since the early '60s) and the carefully tweaked, knowingly retro food – fried school prawns, beef cheek goulash, duck *à l'orange* – adds to the sense of occasion. But you don't get gravitas with your Chateaubriand. Beloved St Kilda painter Mirka Mora's murals grace the wall-infusing all with a rare *joie de vivre*.

⑪ PELICAN *Tapas* $$
☎ 9525 5847; cnr Fitzroy & Park Sts; ☼ breakfast, lunch & dinner; 🚋 16, 96, 112

This modern space evokes beach shacks of days gone by, and makes for a lovely spot to watch the Fitzroy St circus in full swing. Tapas here is not aiming for Iberian authenticity, just good-tasting accompaniments to the drinks menu.

⑪ PIZZA E BIRRA *Italian* $$
☎ 9537 3465; www.pizzaebirra.com .au; 60 Fitzroy St; ☼ lunch Tue-Fri & Sun; 🚋 16, 96

The old train station's great bones and the sharp, graphic (and ever-so-slightly nostalgic) fitout make for a lovely night out. The hand-stretched and wood-fired pizzas (both *tradizionali*, with tomato *sugo*, and *bianche*, without) live up to their surrounds.

⑪ STOKEHOUSE
Modern Australian $$
☎ 9525 5555; www.stokehouse.com .au; 30 Jacka Blvd, St Kilda; ☼ lunch & dinner; 🚋 16, 96

Two-faced Stokehouse makes the most of its beachfront position, cleverly catering to families and drop-ins downstairs, and turning on its best upstairs for finer diners. It's a fixture on the Melbourne dining scene and known for its seafood, service and the bay views on offer. Book for glam upstairs.

⑂ DRINK
⑂ CARLISLE WINE BAR
Wine Bar
☎ 9531 3222; www.carlislewinebar .com.au; 137 Carlisle St, Balaclava; ☼ Mon-Fri 3pm-1am, Sat & Sun 11am-1am; 🚋 Balaclava

Locals love this often rowdy, wine-worshiping former butcher's shop. The staff will treat you like a regular and find you a glass of something special, or effortlessly throw together a cocktail amid the weekend rush. The rustic Euro food (open for brunch on the weekends, dinner daily) is good, too.

⑂ ESPLANADE HOTEL
Live Music
☎ 9534 0211; www.espy.com.au; 11 The Esplanade; 🚋 16, 96

Rock pigs rejoice. The Espy remains gloriously shabby and welcoming to all. Bands play

CARLISLE CAFFEINE

Carlisle St cafes might not catch the sea breeze, but they provide a relaxed pace, local vibe and reliably good coffee. **Batch** (☎ 9530 3550; 320 Carlisle St, Balaclava; 🚊 Balaclava) is run by an ex-Dunedin boy with the Supreme beans and kiwi juices to prove it, while toasted pides and just-right Genovese pull them in to **Wall Two 80** (☎ 9593 8280; rear, 280 Carlisle St, Balaclava; 🚊 Balaclava).

most nights here and there is a spruced-up kitchen out the back. And for the price of a pot you get front-row sunset seats.

▼ GEORGE LANE BAR *Bar*
☎ 9593 8884; www.georgelanebar.com
.au; 1 George Lane (off Grey St); ⏰ 6pm-
1am Wed-Fri, 7pm-1am Sat & Sun;
🚊 96, 16
Hidden behind the hulk of the George Hotel, this little bar is a good rabbit hole to dive into of a night and its pleasantly ad-hoc decor is a relief from the inch-of-its-life design aesthetic elsewhere. There's beer on tap and DJs on the weekends.

▼ MINK *Bar*
☎ 9536 1199; www.minkbar.com.au; 2b
Acland St; ⏰ 9pm-3am; 🚊 16, 96, 112
In this dimly lit trans-Siberian-styled bar, there's no shortage of vodka and glam good times. Get there early to nab the much-sort-after private 'sleeper'.

▼ VINEYARD *Bar*
☎ 9525 4527; 71a Acland St; 🚊 16, 96
The perfect corner position on Acland St and a courtyard barbie

attracts crowds of backpackers and scantily clad young locals who enjoy themselves enough to drown out the neighbouring scenic railway.

⭐ PLAY

▦ AURORA SPA *Spa*
☎ 9536 1130; www.aurorasparetreat
.com; Prince Hotel, 2 Acland St; 🚊 16,
96, 112
This beautiful day spa offers an enormous and creative menu of wellness treatments that go beyond the realm of a massage and a manicure or pedicure. But the staff's tendency to hard-sell on product can rattle after you have just reached a max relaxation mode.

▦ LUNA PARK *Amusement Park*
☎ 9525 5033; www.lunapark.com.au;
Lower Esplanade; adult/child $9.50/7.50
unlimited-ride ticket $41.95/31.95;
⏰ check website for seasonal opening
hours; 🚊 16, 96
It opened in 1912 and still retains the feel of an old-style amusement park with creepy Mr Moon's gap-

ing mouth marking the entrance. There's a heritage-listed scenic railway and a beautiful rococo carousel with hand-painted horses, swans and chariots. For grownups, the noise and lack of greenery or shade can grate after a while.

Resistance sis

⭐ PRINCE BANDROOM

Live Music

☎ 9536 1168; www.princebandroom .com.au; 29 Fitzroy St; 🚋 16, 96, 112

This venue is an institution, and its leafy balcony and raucous downstairs bar are added attractions. Dance acts are a feature but

Exciting amusement ride or sheer lunacy, you decide – Luna Park

JESSICA ROSE

119

THE OLD AND THE NEW

Among the newly minted bars, restaurants and apartments of this reinvented neighbour-hood, there are a few reminders of its not-so-distant bohemian past. The **Esplanade Hotel** (aka the Espy, p117) still adheres to what once was the predominant mood – rock 'n' roll – and the **Galleon Café** (☎ 9534 8934; 9 Carlisle St; 🚊 16, 79, 96) still serves up spanakop-ita and homy puddings to the last of the artists, musicians and writers. **Café Scheherazade** (☎ 9534 2722; 99 Acland St; 🚊 16, 96), famed spinner of schnitzel and creamed spinach dinners, continues to charm a faithful line-up of Eastern European émigrés and more re-cent devoted fans. St Kilda's foodie scene has been bolstered with the arrival of Andrew McConnell's (Culter & Co, Cumulus Inc) Asian restaurant **Golden Fields** (☎ 9525 4488; www.goldenfields.com.au; 157 Fitzroy St; 🚊 16, 96) and the **Newmarket Hotel** (☎ 9537 1777; www.newmarketstkilda.com.au; 34 Inkerman St; 🚊 16, 79).

there's also a good mix of indie, electro-pop, soul and blues.

⭐ ST KILDA SEA BATHS
Swimming Pool
☎ 9525 4888; www.stkildaseabaths.com.au; 10-18 Jacka Blvd; 🚊 16, 96

In the jumble of the Sea Baths building you will find the eponymous seawater pool (it's heated and 25m). There's also a hydrotherapy spa, unisex steam room and magnificent bay views without the brrrrr in winter.

DAWN DELANEY / LONELY PLANET IMAGES
Vintage torque at Torquay, Great Ocean Road (p122)

EXCURSIONS

Twelve Apostles along Shipwreck Coast

MARK PARKES / LONELY PLANET IMAGES ©

GREAT OCEAN ROAD

This stretch of road is worthy of its own Bond film: get ready for some dramatic cliff-side driving. Along with its fabulous views, it's the gateway to pristine hinterland and dotted with laid-back, hospitable towns. Just southwest of Geelong, the Surf Coast town of **Torquay** is the home of many of the world's most loved surf wear and board manufacturers. **Bells Beach**, host of the annual Rip Curl Pro, boasts a must-surf-before-you-die break. Further along, the seascapes grow more breathtaking, matched by amazing coastal architecture; attempt not to look as you take the hairpin turns. The towns of **Anglesea**, **Aireys Inlet**, **Fairhaven** and pretty, but increasingly overdeveloped, **Lorne** offer sustenance (urban coffee standards still apply). The splendid dark forests of the **Otways** and the gently alternative fishing village of **Apollo Bay** will beckon, and can be reached if you're dead keen or happy to stay the night. Keep driving and you're in store for scenic overload, with the **Twelve Apostles** stretching along the **Shipwreck Coast**, set against often stormy skies and the thundering beauty of the Southern Ocean.

INFORMATION
Location Anglesea is 110km southwest of Melbourne
Getting there V/Line buses (☎ 13 61 96; www.vlinepassenger.com.au) run to Lorne. By car, it's two hours via the West Gate Bridge and the Princes Hwy/Torquay–Surf Coast exit.
Contact www.greatoceanrd.org.au

Penguins returning to their nests on Phillip Island

CHRIS MELLOR / LONELY PLANET IMAGES ©

PHILLIP ISLAND

Melburnians come to wild and wind-swept **Phillip Island** to surf or relax in the family-style holiday towns. The 4 million other visitors mostly come for one thing: fairy penguins.

Up to 4000 visitors a night watch as the tiny native penguins waddle from the sea to their nests at sunset. It all happens at Summerland Beach in the **Phillip Island Nature Park** (☎ 5951 2800; Summerland Beach). The visitor information centre is thoughtfully designed to protect the penguins as well as the fragile dunes. Penguin numbers peak in summer, but the parade goes on year-round. You'll need good eyesight – they are the world's smallest penguins. Ranger-led tours are available at extra cost; book ahead for both, especially in summer.

The island also provides other wildlife-watching opportunities. Off the extreme southwestern tip of the island, Australia's largest colony of fur seals – up to 6000 during breeding season – inhabit a group of rocks called the Nobbies. The **Koala Conservation Centre** (☎ 5951 2800; off Phillip Island Rd) lets you peer at koalas from elevated boardwalks at treetop level.

INFORMATION
Location 125km southeast of Melbourne
Getting there V/Line buses (☎ 13 61 96; www.vlinepassenger.com.au) run daily. By car, it's two hours via the Monash Fwy (M1) and South Gippsland Hwy (M420).
Contact www.penguins.org.au

MORNINGTON PENINSULA

The boot-shaped **Mornington Peninsula** – often referred to as simply 'the Peninsula' – is surrounded by water on three sides. This is Melbourne's favourite summer playground. Accordingly, January sees the traffic jams that have temporarily left the city re-form here. It's also chock-a-block come Easter and long weekends.

Facing Port Phillip, the scrubby bay beaches sport bathing boxes, carnivals and a yacht club or two. Oceanside, the southern 'back' beaches are magnificent, though often too ferocious or freezing for a casual paddle. The towns become more upmarket as you travel down the bay, with huge, gated properties and helipads gracing the foreshore beyond **Sorrento**. For a pot and a pub meal with a wonderful view of the pier, grab a garden table at the **Portsea Hotel** (☎ 5984 2213; www.portseahotel.com.au; Point Nepean Rd).

Overlooking Western Port Bay, you'll find rocky, tree-clad beaches and a string of decidedly calmer hamlets. These towns are also in swilling and spitting distance of a hundred or so of Victoria's best wine-producers. Pinot Grigio and Chardonnay grapes love the cool, maritime climate; pinot noir is also produced, and there are plantings of newer Italian aromatics.

The Peninsula's elevated centre is remarkably bucolic, with villages tucked between rolling hills and bushland. A soak in the outdoor **Peninsula Hot Springs** (☎ 5950 8777; www.peninsulahotsprings.com; Springs Lane, Rye; ⏲ 7.30am-10pm) is a must-do. Visit the monthly **Red Hill Community Market** (☎ 5974 4710; Red Hill Recreation Reserve; ⏲ 8am-1pm 1st Sat, Sep-May). Grab a pizza and a Pinot Gris at perennially popular **T'Gallant Vineyard** (☎ 5931 1300; www.tgallant. com.au; 1385 Mornington Flinders Rd, Main Ridge) or get a local culinary surprise at **Merricks General Store** (☎ 5989 8088; www.mgwinestore.com.au; 3460 Frankston-Flinders Rd, Merricks) where you'll meet legendary local winemaker Kathleen Quealy and, come winter, get the opportunity to go mushroom hunting.

INFORMATION

Location 90km southeast of Melbourne
Getting there Take the freeway from the Nepean Hwy or the more scenic Point Nepean Rd by exiting at Mornington. Via the freeway, the trip from Melbourne takes just over an hour.
Contact www.visitmorningtonpeninsula.org

DANDENONGS & THE YARRA VALLEY

The **Dandenong Ranges** rise from the suburban sprawl directly to the east of the city. Melbourne's backyard is a world of giant ancient ferns and kooky tearooms, English-style flower gardens and native lyrebirds. To the north is the town of **Healesville**, more rustic than quaint, but boasting a flash cellar door/bakery at **Innocent Bystander** (☎ 5962 6111; www .innocentbystander.com.au; 336 Maroondah Hwy) and, next door, **White Rabbit brewery** (☎ 5962 6516; www.whiterabbitbeer.com.au; 316 Maroondah Hwy, Healesville), where you can go for tastings of the amber liquid. The **Healesville Wildlife Sanctuary** (☎ 5957 2800; www.zoo.org.au/healesvillesanctuary; Badger Creek Rd) is brilliant if you've discovered that kangaroos don't wander down Bourke St and are keen to catch up with some native animals without going bush. Plus the platypus home and viewing enclosure are stunning, as is the new visitor information centre. Pop into the wonderful **TarraWarra Museum of Art** (☎ 5957 3100; twma.com.au; 311 Healesville-Yarra Glen Rd) or continue to the **Yarra Valley** proper. Neat lines of vineyards stretch for kilometres and gradually give way to tangles of bush. This famed wine region turns out top quality cool climate sparklings, Cab Savs, Pinot Noir and Chardonnays. Restaurants with vineyard views abound, from the big guns such as **Yering Station** (☎ 9730 0100; www.yering.com; 38 Melba Hwy, Yarra Glen) to boutique producers like **Bianchet** (☎ 9739 1779; www.bianchetwinery.com.au; 187 Victoria Rd, Lilydale).

INFORMATION
Location Healesville is 60km northeast of Melbourne
Getting there Catch the Lilydale train from Flinders St, then a connecting bus to Healesville. By car, it's 50 minutes via the Maroondah Hwy.
Contact www.wineyarravalley.com

>SNAPSHOTS

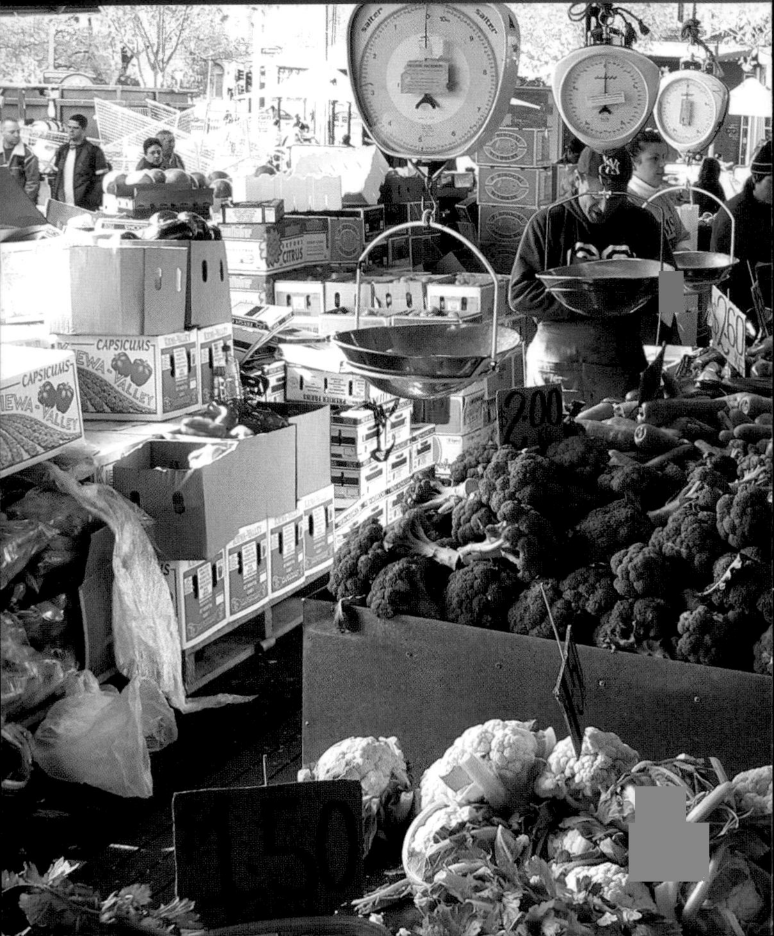

Whether you've come to eat your fill and stay out late, contemplate contemporary art or spur on a sporting team to victory, Melbourne will delight, inspire and excite. The city excels on style, spectacle and substance; whatever your mood you'll find something to suit.

SALLY DARMODY

Always a hive of activity – the Queen Victoria Market (p40)

> ACCOMMODATION

While you'll have no trouble finding a place to stay that suits your taste and budget, Melbourne has surprisingly few truly inspirational boltholes and only a handful of atmospheric, individual small hotels. Still, prices are rarely stratospheric and across the board, quality is high.

For a standard double room in a deluxe hotel, expect to pay upwards of $350. For a top-end room you'll pay between $250 and $300, midrange around $150 and for a budget double, around $80 to $100. Prices peak during the Australian Open in January, Grand Prix weekend in March, during AFL finals in September and Spring Racing Carnival in November. Midrange to deluxe hotels publish 'rack rates', but always ask for current specials and for inclusions such as breakfast or parking. All accommodation has a 10% goods and services tax (GST) included in the price.

Apartment-style accommodation is easy to find in Melbourne – there are several local as well as national chains – and suits those that want a smart, functional space to relax and stow their shopping but don't need full hotel accoutrements. There are also plenty of budget hostels, pubs and B&Bs. Many big hostels offer private rooms and basic dorms.

Take a look at Melbourne's neighbourhood layout before deciding where to rest your head. The city will please everyone. If you like to take a morning stroll in something resembling nature, choose somewhere towards Spring St for easy access to Fitzroy Gardens, or close to Flinders St or on Southbank for a riverside run. East Melbourne is good for peace and quiet with city proximity. Docklands will give you great, if industrial,

Need a place to stay? Find and book it at lonelyplanet. com. Over 200 properties are featured for Melbourne – each personally visited, thoroughly reviewed and happily recommended by a Lonely Planet author. From hostels to high-end hotels, we've hunted out the places that will bring you unique and special experiences. Read independent reviews by authors and other travellers, and get practical information including amenities, maps and photos. Then reserve your room simply and securely via Hotels & Hostels – our online booking service. It's all at lonelyplanet.com/hotels.

views of Victoria Harbour and the city, and has its own swag of dining options, but it can be a pain to make your way back to the midcity action. South of the river, South Yarra has a number of boutique and up-market places set in pretty tree-lined residential streets. You'll be close to shopping, parkland and some sort of nightlife. Further south, St Kilda is a hotel hub with one of the city's most famed boutique hotels and a budget-traveller enclave. Although bay views can be found, don't count on them – the beach, however, is usually only a short walk away. Fitzroy hums with attractions day and night, and a few interesting sleeping options have popped up in the past few years.

WEB RESOURCES

Tourism Victoria's website, Visit Melbourne (www.visitmelbourne.com), has an accommodation listing section with a comprehensive range of budgets, but no direct booking service. Global discounters such as www.wotif.com.au have a good inventory of mainstream hotels and apartments, often with substantial savings on deluxe city places at weekends.

BEST FOR SHOPPING & BAR HOPPING
> Adelphi Hotel (www.adelphi.com.au)
> Hotel Lindrum (www.hotellindrum.com.au)
> Medina Executive Flinders Street (www.medina.com.au)
> Olsen (www.artserieshotels.com.au/olsen)
> Tyrian Serviced Apartments (www.tyrian.com.au)

BEST LEAFY BOUTIQUE HOTELS
> Albany (www.thealbany.com.au)
> Hatton (www.hatton.com.au)
> Lyall Hotel (www.thelyall.com)
> Villa Donati (www.villadonati.com)

BEST TOP-ENDERS
> Hilton Melbourne South Wharf (www.hiltonmelbourne.com.au)
> Sofitel Melbourne on Collins (www.sofitelmelbourne.com.au)

BEST BAYSIDE DIGS
> Cosmopolitan Hotel (www.cosmopolitanhotel.com.au)
> Hotel Tolarno (www.hoteltolarno.com.au)
> Prince (www.theprince.com.au)

BEST HOSTELS
> Melbourne Central Hostel (www.yha.com.au)
> Nunnery (www.nunnery.com.au)

SNAPSHOTS

> FOOD

Melburnians have often grown up with at least one other culinary culture besides the rather grim Anglo-Australian fare of mid-last-century. This makes for a city of adventurous, if often highly critical, palates. Melbourne's food scene is one of almost limitless choice; there is a constant flow of new ideas, new places and reinvention.

At the top of the food chain, fine diners thrive. While many Melbourne chefs experiment widely, mixing and matching technique and ingredient, you'll rarely find chefs doing fusion for fusion's sake. You'll instead find menus that rove across regions and riff on influences. There are those who head in a contemporary French direction, such as Shannon Bennett at Vue de Monde (p47) and Ben Shewry at Attica, but you're more likely to see a thoughtful pan-Mediterranean menu. Others incorporate both modern Mediterranean and Asian ideas and flavours to greater or lesser degrees; Andrew McConnell at Fitzroy's Cutler & Co (p98) and the city centre's Cumulus Inc (p45) manages to create a particularly thoughtful but easy-going version of this style, with Pearl (p86) upping the Asian flavours. There's a long tradition of posh Italian dining in the city, and it's often exemplary with chefs like Guy Grossi at Grossi Florentino. Eastern Mediterranean is done with five-star flair and a modern sensibility by Greg Malouf at MoMo and George Calombaris at the Press Club (p47).

Given that there's so much to try, Melburnians love to eat out often. The city really shines when it comes to a more informal, grazing style of dining, and you'll find quality produce and attention to detail don't flag. Small and large plates override the standard three-course chronology, flavours sing and everyone digs in. Bar food is no longer seen as a mere consort to booze, it's an equal marriage of tastes and experiences.

Cafes are an integral part of life, with many Melburnians up early so they can catch up with colleagues (or just the newspaper) for a coffee and spot of breakfast before the work day begins. Coffee quality is hotly debated; everyone has a favourite roaster and barista. A drab lunch sandwich is a thing of the past: piadinas, panini, tarts and sushi have filled the gap. Along with the Queen Victoria Market and its suburban counterparts in South Melbourne and Prahran, there is a weekly rota of **farmers markets** (www.mfm.com.au), which bring local suppliers and fresh produce to town. And locals love them for a Saturday morning coffee and food-related stroll.

Melbourne's ethnic cuisines were once tightly zoned, and although now spread widely over the city, there are still dedicated clusters. Richmond's Victoria St is packed with Vietnamese restaurants and providores; the western suburb of Footscray also draws those looking for the most authentic Vietnamese (as well as great African) food. Lygon St, Carlton, has long been home to simple red-sauce Italian cooking, with a few notable innovators, and the coffee and delis are great. Chinatown is home to one of Australia's most renowned restaurants of any culinary persuasion, the **Flower Drum** (Map pp36-7, F3; ☎ 9662 3655; 17 Market Lane, Melbourne). You'll find regional gems such as **Dainty Sichuan** (Map pp36-7, F2; ☎ 9663 8861; 26 Corrs Lane, Melbourne) as well as Japanese, Malaysian and Korean here, too. One street up, Lonsdale St has a handful of Greek taverna and bars. The northern suburb of Brunswick has a number of wonderful Middle Eastern bakers and grocers as well as cafes. What's off the boil? Thai food often lacks the zing that's found in Sydney, there's not a lot of upmarket Indian to be had and, at the time of writing, nothing in the way of Modern Scando. But it's only a matter of time.

The Melbourne Food & Wine Festival (see p21) in March is a highlight for gourmets and hungry amateurs alike, and the city's best restaurants offer fixed-price lunches for a steal. The *Age* newspaper publishes a weekly food and wine supplement on Tuesdays, as well as the annual *Good Food Guide* and its companion *Cheap Eats*. Many of the restaurant reviews can be found on the newspaper's website (www.theage.com.au).

BEST CASUAL DINING

> Bar Lourinhã (p44)
> Cumulus Inc (p45)
> Earl Canteen (p45)
> Hutong Dumpling Bar (p45)

BEST PIZZA

> Ladro (p99)
> Meine Liebe (p100)
> Pizza e Birra (p117)

BEST FINE DINERS

> Circa at the Prince (p115)
> Cutler & Co (p98)
> Press Club (p47)
> Vue de Monde (p47)

> DRINKING

Melbourne's thriving bar scene is one of its biggest attractions. When liquor licensing laws were liberalised in the late 1980s, bars began to spring up anywhere rent was cheap and space was atmospheric. Many were opened by artists, architects or young hospitality workers and fitted out with creative verve in lieu of huge wads of cash. Today, that spirit of invention still persists even if the stakes are higher. No one is sure just how many bars the city can sustain, but the scene shows no sign of letting up anytime soon.

The same legislation also made it easy for cafes and restaurants to serve alcohol, an idea common enough throughout Europe, but one still quite foreign to many Australian cites. This has meant the boundaries between what constitutes a restaurant, bar or cafe are gloriously blurred. The place you take your morning short black could quite easily be somewhere you find yourself dancing to Cut Copy come 1am. Neighbourhoods like St Kilda, Prahran and Fitzroy each have their own versions of the city bar, and shopfront fitouts fan out into the suburbs following the hip kids to neighbourhoods such as Brunswick, Northcote and Yarraville.

MICHAEL RUFF

The bar revolution has ironically done nothing to dim the appeal of the neighbourhood pub, though it has meant that most have had to do some rethinking and some judicious refurbishing. And while Melburnians still profess to love a good old-fashioned boozer, they're often secretly pleased when their local offers Mornington Peninsula wines by the glass and keeps a few different vodkas chilled in the fridge.

Most bars and pubs stay open until midnight or beyond, but it's always worth checking ahead for opening hours if you're planning a late one. Beer is taken seriously in Melbourne and most places serve a variety of local, boutique and imported beers on tap, as well as a wider range by the bottle. Beer is ordered by the pot or pint. Cocktails are increasingly made with skill and premium ingredients, with prices to match. Wine is served by the glass and the bottle, and it's now common to find European wines. Smoking is banned in all bars and pubs, though there will often be a balcony or courtyard provided.

With many bars concealed up an anonymous flight of stairs, down an alley off a back street, or tucked along a riverbank (such as Riverland, pictured left), how does a visitor keep up? Melburnians are normally more proud than proprietorial about their favourites, so it's always worth asking a barman or fellow drinker at somewhere you've already discovered. Bar reviews can be found on the *Age* newspaper's website and Three Thousand (www.threethousand.com.au) keeps a pretty close eye on the latest places to pop up.

BEST WINE BARS
> Carlisle Wine Bar (p117)
> City Wine Shop (p49)
> Gerald's Bar (p110)
> Gertrude St Enoteca (p100)

BEST PUBS
> Carlton Hotel (p48)
> Miss Libertine (p52)
> Prince Bandroom (p119)
> Union Club Hotel (p101)

BEST COCKTAILS
> 1806 (p48)
> Berlin Bar (p48)
> Cavallero (p97)
> Seamstress (p47)
> Toff in Town (p52)

BEST UNMARKED BARS
> George Lane Bar (p118)
> New Gold Mountain (p51)
> Panama Dining Room (p99)

> FASHION

Melburnians like to look good; fashion is important. Office clobber may have become more relaxed, and going-out clothes more casual too, but this just gives everyone more opportunities to improvise and layer. The city is catered by an impressive number of canny retailers who roam widely in search of the world's best as well as showcasing local design talent. And there's lots of that. Rather than adhering to the hierarchy of established studios, many young designers start their own labels straight out of university. This gives the scene an amazing energy and vitality. There are also a large number who have their own flagship shops, where the designer's particular look and personality is writ large and whole collections can be discovered.

Melbourne's designers are known for their tailoring, luxury fabrics, innovation and blending of global elements, all underscored with a fuss-free Australian sensibility. Those to watch out for include the evergreen Scanlan & Theodore and TL Wood for smart, lyrical elegance; Tony Maticevki and Martin Grant for demi-couture and dark reworkings of the classics; Ess Hoshika, Dhini and Munk for conceptual, deconstructed pieces; Anna Thomas and Vixen for the luxuriously grown-up, either tailored (Thomas) or flowing (Vixen); Gorman, Arabella Ramsay and Obüs for hipster cheek with a delightfully feminine twist; Alpha60 and Claude Maus for clever, urban pieces; Mjölk for precision-cut menswear; and, finally, scene stalwarts Bettina Liano for straight-ahead glamour and Alannah Hill for the original girly-girl layers.

One constant is colour, or lack of it. You'll not go long in Melbourne without hearing mention of 'Melbourne black', and it's true that inky shades are worn winter, spring, summer and autumn. Perhaps it's because it works well with the soft light and often grey days, or maybe it's a product of many Melburnians' southern European heritage. It could be the subliminal influence of the city's building blocks of moody bluestone. Some speculate that it's the lingering fallout of the explosive 1980s post-punk scene. The fact is black clothes sell far better here than in any other city in the country, and it's hard to succeed as a designer if you don't add a little every season. It's never out of fashion.

Where to shop? The city has national and international chains spread out over Bourke and Collins Sts, as well as the city malls of Melbourne Central, QV, GPO and Australia on Collins. Smaller shops and designer workshops inhabit the laneways and vertical villages of Curtin House and the Nicholas Building. A strip of Little Collins is dedicated to sartorially savvy gentlemen. The length of leafy Collins St is lined with luxury retailers, especially towards its Spring St end. Chapel St also has many of the chains and classic Australian designers, as well as some interesting players at the Prahran end. Further up the hill, hit Hawksburn Village (see boxed text, p76) or High St, Armadale (see boxed text, p74), for bobo (bourgeois bohemian) chic and fashion forward labels. Greville St and Windsor do streetwear. Lygon St, Carlton, has some great small shops specialising in European tailoring and local talent, while Brunswick St does streetwear and pulses with the energy of young designers in stores such as the legendary Fat. Gertrude St mixes vintage with the innovators as well as some great menswear. This is just the tip of the well-cut iceberg, with fashion popping up in many other neighbourhoods as well.

KYLIE MCLAUGHLIN / LONELY PLANET IMAGES ©

BEST LOCAL DESIGNER SHOPS

> Alphaville (p91)
> Gorman (p92)
> Signet Bureau (p94)
> TL Wood (p76)

BEST BOUTIQUES

> Alice Euphemia (p41)
> Christine (p41)
> ESS (p92)
> Marais (p43; pictured above)
> Spacecraft (p94)

> ART

You'll be missing the point if you come to Melbourne expecting exhaustive troves of old masters and key Modernist pieces. Melbourne's art world revolves around innovation and experimentation, and collections reflect both the youth and isolation of the city. Museums are strong on contemporary work, as well as indigenous art and Australian impressionism. Dealers have found themselves part of a global explosion in the art market, but also have noted the growing sophistication of local collectors.

Flinders Lane has the densest concentration of commercial galleries in Australia, and there are others dotted throughout the city and in Fitzroy, Richmond, Prahran, South Yarra and St Kilda. Artist-run spaces also thrive in these neighbourhoods and out into the suburbs. These include Platform, Conical, Kings Artist Run Initiative, Seventh Gallery and West Space.

GERARD WALKER / LONELY PLANET IMAGES ©

Notable midcareer Melbourne artists include Callum Morton, Stephen Bram, Daniel Von Sturmer and Natasha Johns-Messenger for work that investigates physical space; Nick Mangan, Patricia Piccinini and Ricky Swallow for sculptural pieces that distort the everyday; Matthew Johnson, Kerry Poliness and Melinda Harper for work that uses pattern and draws on traditional painting and drawing techniques to variously seduce, evoke and question; and John Young, Brook Andrew and Constanze Zikos for work that examines their respective cultural heritage via complex plays of abstraction and representation.

Of course, there's a whole other generation hot on their heels. As well as making use of the city's artist studio programs, such as those at Gertrude Contemporary Art Spaces (p90), and the network of artist-run spaces, many emerging artists blur art, craft and design boundaries. They often exhibit and sell their work through shops and markets, such as the weekly **Rose Street Artists Market** (Map p89, A2; www.rosestmarket.com.au; 60 Rose St, Fitzroy; 🕒 11am-5pm Sat & Sun). Art can also be found outside the gallery in a huge range of public art initiatives; many are listed on the City of Melbourne's website (www.melbourne.vic.gov.au). Look to *Art Almanac* (www.art-almanac.com.au) for gallery listings and the 'A2' section or magazine in Saturday's *Age* for reviews. Also see p10 for more on the explosion of street art in Melbourne's laneways.

BEST ART SPACES
> Australian Centre for Contemporary Art (p56)
> Australian Centre for the Moving Image (p38)
> Heide Museum of Modern Art (p90; pictured left, *Rings of Saturn*, Inge King)
> Ian Potter Centre: NGV Australia (p38)
> Ian Potter Museum of Art (p103)
> National Gallery of Victoria International (p56)

BEST COMMERCIAL GALLERIES
> Anna Schwartz Gallery (p38)
> Alcaston Gallery (p90)
> Sutton Gallery (p91)
> Utopian Slumps (p41)

> ARCHITECTURE

For a planned city, and a relatively youthful one, Melbourne's street-scapes are richly textured. Long considered one of the world's most beautiful Victorian cities, Melbourne captures the spirit of that age. There's exuberantly embellished Second Empire institutions and hulking former factories that would make Manchester proud. Gems from the 19th century include the Princess Theatre (p53), by William Pitt; the Royal Exhibition Building (p103), the State Library of Victoria (p40; pictured below), Melbourne Town Hall and Trades Hall, by Joseph Reed; and the Windsor Hotel and Royal Arcade, by Charles Webb.

Flinders St Station and the original Queen Victoria Hospital building at the QV herald in the Federation era, when a new Australian identity was being fashioned from the fetching combination of red brick and ornate wood. Look down Swanston St from Lonsdale St and you'll catch a glimpse of a mini-Manhattan. Melbourne's between-the-wars optimism is captured in its string of stunning, if somewhat stunted, art deco skyscrapers such as the Manchester Unity Building. Walter Burley Griffin worked in the city at this time too, creating the ornate, organic Newman College at the University of Melbourne and the mesmerising ode to the metropolitan, the Capitol Theatre (p53).

RICHARD NEBESKY / LONELY PLANET IMAGES ©

By the mid-20th century, modernist architects sought new ways to connect with the local landscape as well as honouring the movement's internationalist roots; the most prominent, Roy Grounds, designed the Arts Centre and the original NGV on St Kilda Rd. Others include Robin Boyd, Kevin Borland and Alistair Knox; their work is mostly residential and rarely open to the public. You can, however, visit a beautiful Boyd anytime: Jimmy Watson's (p110) wine bar in Carlton. Melbourne also had its own midcentury furniture design stars, Grant and Mary Featherston, whose iconic Contour chair of 1951 is highly prized by collectors, as are their '70s modular sofas.

The 1990s saw a flurry of public building works. Melbourne's architects fell in love with technology and designed with unorthodox shapes, vibrant colours, tactile surfaces and blatantly sexy structural features. Denton Corker Marshall's Melbourne Museum (p103), Melbourne Convention & Exhibition Centre, Bolte Bridge and CityLink sound tunnel are emblematic. Federation Sq, one of the last of these major projects, continues to polarise opinion. Despite the detractors, its cobbled piazza has become the city's centre of celebration and protest, surely the best compliment a populace can pay an architect. Ashton Raggatt McDougall's Melbourne Recital Centre is a recent architectural prize winner.

Melbourne's architectural energy today comes not from the monumental but from what goes on in-between the new and the old, the towering and the tiny. Midcareer practices such as Six Degrees, Ellenberg Fraser and Kerstin Thompson create witty, inventive and challenging buildings and interiors that see these spaces spring to life.

Philip Goad's *Guide to Melbourne Architecture* and the *Melbourne Design Guide*, edited by Viviane Stappmanns and Ewan McEoin, are excellent resources. Visit **Architext Bookshop** (Map pp36-7, G4; ☎ 8620 3815; www.architext.com.au; 76 Flinders Lane, Melbourne) for more.

BEST BUILDINGS
> Melbourne Museum (p103)
> National Gallery of Victoria International (p56)
> Parliament House (p40)
> State Library of Victoria (p40)

BEST INTERIORS
> Cumulus Inc (p45)
> Cutler & Co (p98)
> Hilton Melbourne South Wharf (p129)
> New Gold Mountain (p51)

> SPORT

Underneath the cultured chat and designer threads of your typical Melburnian, you'll find a heart that truly belongs to one thing: sport. The city takes the shared spectacle and tribal drama of the playing field very seriously; at the same time, it's also a lot of fun. Jump into a taxi at Melbourne Airport and the conversation will no doubt begin…

Understanding the basics of Australian Rules football (AFL, or just 'the footy') is definitely a way to get a local engaged in conversation, especially during the winter season. But you'll often find their interest wanders across code and game as well.

Soccer's popularity is on the rise; Melbourne Victory's supporter base is enthusiastic enough to warrant the building of a brand new home ground, the brilliantly lit AAMI Park, which is shared by Super Rugby team the Melbourne Rebels and successful Rugby League team Melbourne Storm. There's no local pro rugby union comp, but the occasional international tests played in Melbourne draw huge, enthusiastic crowds and tickets invariably sell out months in advance. The Melbourne Storm rugby league team won the 2007 NRL trophy, and the team has a small, but fanatically loyal and growing, supporter base.

The infectious energy that surrounds the Australian Open in January reveals a deeply tennis-mad city. Melbourne's other summer love is cricket. The Boxing Day Test is bigger than Christmas and later in January, capacity day–night matches under the lights at the MCG often combine great sporting moments with equally newsworthy crowd exploits.

Enthusiastic spectators, Melburnians are also fond of working up a sweat themselves. They love to whack the little white ball, and both public and private golf courses abound. Cape Schanck is a particularly scenic links around 1½ hours' drive from town. Cycling is a way of life for many who take advantage of the city's extensive network of bike paths and scant hills to commute during the week or relax on weekends. There's a dynamic club scene with weekend rides followed by lycra-clad cafe breakfasts. Yachties take to Port Phillip Bay; there's a string of bayside sailing clubs. The closest ski fields can be reached in under three hours, and although snow falls have become increasingly erratic over the last few years, when the powder falls, it's just possible for a day trip. Surfers make the 1½-hour trek to either the Mornington Peninsula or the Surf Coast for some of the world's best, if chilly, waves.

> GAY & LESBIAN

Melbourne's gay and lesbian scene might often be overlooked in favour of Sydney's raucously out and proud one, but it thrives regardless and suits many who prefer things a little less commercialised. Although there are a couple of distinctly pink neighbourhoods that are definitely on the dance card, demarcation isn't a big thing. Most inner-city venues are mixed and completely nondiscriminatory.

Commercial Rd, South Yarra, is most gay visitors' first point of call. There's a cluster of high-energy bars, cafes and clubs catering predominantly to men, but also to women. In St Kilda, the Prince Bandroom (p119) hosts the monthly Girlbar (www.girlbar.com.au). Below, in the Prince of Wales proper, the saloon bar has a jukebox, with lipsyncing comps and half-price beer on Monday. The Greyhound Hotel does drag on the weekends. North of the river, the scene is dotted around pubs and clubs in Collingwood and Abbotsford; it's a little more laid-back and alternative. Venues to look out for are the **Peel** (Map p89, C4; ☎ 9419 4762; www.thepeel.com.au; cnr Peel & Wellington Sts, Collingwood), the **Glasshouse** (Map p89, C3; ☎ 9419 4748; www.myglasshouse.com.au; 51 Gipps St, Collingwood) and the biker/bear-friendly **Laird** (Map p89, D4; ☎ 9417 2832; www.lairdhotel.com; 149 Gipps St, Abbotsford), which also has accommodation. You'll also find **Hares & Hyenas Bookshop** (Map p89, A2; ☎ 9495 6589; www.hares-hyenas.com.au; 63 Johnston St, Fitzroy).

Up-to-date listings of venues and club nights can be found in the free *Southern Star* (www.staroberver.com.au) and *MCV* (mcv.gaynewsnetwork .com.au), both distributed in cafes, bars and clubs. Fabulous Joy FM (94.9FM; www.joy.org.au) pumps out the party tunes and has specialist programming for all sections of the gay, lesbian, bisexual, transgender and intersex community. Visitors looking for gay- and lesbian-operated accommodation should check out the **GALstays website** (www.galstays.com.au), which has a range of guesthouses and B&Bs. Another accommodation directory for gay and lesbian travellers is **qbeds** (www.qbeds.com.au).

> PARKS & GARDENS

Melbourne's city grid is looped in a belt of green. In a city not blessed with dramatic geography, this extensive network of parks and gardens has created a variety of landscapes and natural places for Melburnians to relax and reconnect with nature.

The 19th-century colonists found Melbourne's original plants and trees unvarying and impermeable, and were hell-bent on imposing a familiar aesthetic upon their new home. This colonial hubris has had its upside, bestowing upon Melbourne a notable European, and largely British, botanical heritage. At the same time, there is a ground-swell of interest in restoring as well as re-creating the city's original landscape, and you'll find parks with thriving indigenous plantings. There is also a profound awareness of the environmental cost of maintaining parks and gardens – especially those filled with plants more suited to the climate of Kent or Surrey – in drought-ravaged times. If you find less-than-emerald expanses of lawn, empty fountains and the odd sight of orange plastic barricades drip feeding wilting elm trees, you'll understand why.

Melburnians make use of their precious parks to kick a ball (both round and egg-shaped), cycle, jog, meet friends for a picnic or simply for a quick kip under a tree at lunchtime (there's more than 50,000 of these to choose from in the city alone). The parks also make for a very pleasant commute to the city for lucky inner-city residents. Many parks offer well-maintained gas barbecue faciltes that are coin operated. Contact **Melbourne City Council** (☎ 9658 9658; www.melbourne.vic.gov.au) and **Parks Victoria** (☎ 13 19 63; www.parkweb.vic.gov.au) for more information.

BEST BOTANICAL HERITAGE
> Royal Botanic Gardens (p71)
> Fitzroy Gardens (p81)

BEST INDIGENOUS GARDENS
> Birrarung Marr (p38)
> Herring Island (p71)
> Royal Park (Trin Warren Tam-boore; p111)

PETER LESLIE

Indigenous performance of a sacred ceremony

BACKGROUND

INDIGENOUS MELBOURNE

In the Dreaming, the land and the people were created by the spirit Bunjil – 'the great one, old head-man, eagle hawk' – who continues to watch over the Wurundjeri from Tharangalk-bek, the home of the spirits in the sky. The land is entrusted to the people, and they carry a sacred pact to welcome visitors.

The catchment of the Yarra River has been home to the Wurundjeri-willem people for at least 45,000 years. The Wurundjeri were a tribe of the Woiworung, one of five distinct language groups belonging to the Kulin Nation. They often traded and celebrated among the towering red gums, tea trees and ferns of the river's edge with their coastal counterparts the Bunnerong, as well as the clans from the north and west.

As the flood-prone rivers and creeks broke their banks in winter, bark shelters would be built north in the ranges. Possums were hunted for their meat and skinned to make calf-length cloaks. Worn with fur against skin, the smooth outer hide was rubbed with waterproofing fat and embellished with totemic designs: graphic chevrons and diamonds or representations of emus and kangaroos. During the summer, camps were made along the Yarra, the Maribyrnong and Merri Creek. Food – from slow-roasted kangaroo, waterfowl, fish and eel, to grubs, yam daisies and banksia-blossom cordial – was plentiful. Wurundjeri men and women were compelled to marry out of the tribe, requiring complex forms of diplomacy. Ceremonies and bouts of ritual combat were frequent.

In 1835, when John Batman arrived from Van Diemen's Land, he travelled through 'beautiful land…rather sandy, but the sand black and rich, covered with kangaroo grass about ten inches high and as green as a field of wheat'. He noted stone dams for catching fish built across creeks, trees that bore the scars of bark harvesting and women bearing wooden water containers and woven bags holding stone tools. The Wurundjeri's profound relationship with the land and intimate knowledge of story, ceremony and season would be irrevocably damaged within a few short years. European diseases and a polluted water supply killed many of those who continued to camp by the Yarra. Despite enormous pressures and provocation, the Wurundjeri rarely resorted to violence against the Europeans. As the settlement of Melbourne transmogrified from pastoral outpost to heaving, gold-rush metropolis in scarcely 30 years,

---

CONNECTING WITH INDIGENOUS CULTURE

Places to connect with indigenous culture:

> **Koori Heritage Trust** (p39) Take a Walkin' Birrarung tour along the Yarra and explore the vibrant natural and cultural landscape beneath the modern city.
> **Bunjilaka at the Melbourne Museum** (p103) See and experience cultural heritage items interpreted via Aboriginal voices.
> **Royal Botanic Garden's Aboriginal Heritage Walk** (p162) Share in the wealth of local plant lore and see the landscape through the eyes of an Aboriginal guide.
> **Charcoal Lane** (p97) Taste bush foods prepared with contemporary flair.

---

the cumulative effects of dispossession, alcohol and increasing acts of violence saw a shocking decline in Melbourne's indigenous population.

From the earliest days, the colonial authorities evicted Wurundjeri and other Kulin people from their lands. In 1863 the Board for the Protection of Aborigines led a band of a few dozen Wurundjeri survivors to a Presbyterian mission on the upper Yarra. 'Coranderrk' became a self-sufficient farming community and allowed the inhabitants a measure of 'independence', along with twice-daily prayers and new boots at Christmas. In the 1870s eugenicist government policies meant that those of mixed blood could not remain in the reserve and, as great numbers were evicted, it became unviable. The Wurundjeri were again moved on, this time to the four corners of Victoria.

Despite this, the Wurundjeri have survived. Melbourne has a indigenous population of around 15,000, some of whom are of direct Kulin Nation descent. They continue to live, practice and renew their culture to this day.

POSTSETTLEMENT HISTORY
BOLD AS BEARBRASS

1803: it wasn't an auspicious start. With a missed mail ship communiqué and a notoriously supercilious British government calling the shots, Surveyor-General Charles Grimes' recommendations that the best place to found a southern French-foiling settlement would be by the banks of the 'Freshwater River' (aka the Yarra) went unheeded. The chosen alternative, Sorrento, was an unmitigated disaster from the start. As Lieutenant David Collins pointed out to his superiors, you can't survive long without drinkable water. (For one extremely tenacious convict escapee, William Buckley, it wasn't all bad: he survived to see John Batman turn up a few decades later.)

Australian-born John Batman, an arriviste grazier from Van Diemen's Land, sailed into Port Phillip Bay in mid-1835 with an illegal contract of sale. (The British government's colonial claims relied on the fiction that the original inhabitants did not own the land on which they lived, and hence could not sell it.) He sought out some local chiefs and on a tributary of the Yarra – it's been speculated that it was Merri Creek, in today's Northcote – found some 'fine-looking' men, with whom he exchanged blankets, scissors, mirrors and handkerchiefs for a half million acres of land surrounding Port Phillip. Despite the fact that the Sydney Aborigines accompanying Batman couldn't speak a word of the local language and vice versa, Batman brokered the deal and signatures were gathered from the local chiefs (all suspiciously called Jika-Jika and with remarkably similar penmanship). He noted a low rocky falls several kilometres up the Yarra (about where the Queen St Bridge is today). This upstream fresh water made it 'a perfect place for a village'.

Batman then returned to Tasmania to ramp up the Port Phillip Association. It's at this point in the historical narrative that things get as turbid as the Yarra itself. Before he managed to return to the new settlement, which he called Bearbrass (along with 'Yarra', another cocksure misappropriation of the local dialect), John Pascoe Fawkner, a Launceston publican, got wind of the spectacular opportunity. He promptly sent off a small contingent of settlers aboard the schooner *Enterprize,* who upon arrival got to building huts and establishing a garden. On Batman's return there were words, and later furious bidding wars, over allotments of land. Called variously 'a visionary' and 'a sanctimonious little prick' by historians, Fawkner's place in history was sealed by the fact he outlived the syphilitic Batman by several decades. Whatever the interpersonal politics between the wannabe founders, the settlement grew quickly; around a year later, almost 200 brave souls (and some tens of thousands of sheep) had thrown their lot in with the two Johnnies.

New South Wales wasn't happy. Governor Bourke dispatched Captain William Lonsdale in 1836 and dispelled any notion of ownership by the Port Phillip Association. This was crown land; surveyors were sent for to draw up plans for a city. Robert Hoddle, Surveyor in Charge, arrived with the Governor in March 1837, and began to reign in his unruly staff (they had absconded up river to get drunk or shoot kangaroos one too many times) and the antipodean topography. For Hoddle, it was all about straight lines. Hoddle's grid, demarcated by the Yarra and what was once a 'hillock' where Southern Cross Station now lies, is Melbourne's defining feature. Land sales commenced almost immediately; surveying continued with little romantic notion of exploration or discovery. It was, by all accounts, a real-estate feeding frenzy. The British were well served by their 'terra nullius' concept; returns on investment were fabulous. The rouseabout Bearbrass was upgraded to 'Melbourne', after the serving British prime minister. Various kings, queens and assorted contemporary bigwigs (including Governor Bourke himself) got the nod when naming central streets. By 1840 the place, with 10,000 occasionally upstanding citizens, was looking decidedly civilised.

GOLDEN YEARS

In 1840 a local landowner described the fledgling city as 'a goldfield without the gold'. Indeed, with a steady stream of immigrants and confidence-building prosperity, there had been growing calls for separation from convict-ridden, rowdy New South Wales. By the end of 1850, the newly minted colony of Victoria had got its go-it-alone wish. This quickly seemed like a cruel stroke of fate; gold was discovered near Bathurst in New South Wales in early 1851. Pastoral riches or not, there was every chance that without a viable labour force (many had already succumbed to the siren call CALIFORN-I-A!) the colony would wither and die. Melbourne jewellers had for some time been doing a clandestine trade with shepherds who came to town with small, illegally got nuggets secreted in their kerchiefs. Wary of the consequences for civic order, but with few other options, the city's leading men declared that gold must be found. A committee was formed, a reward was offered. Slim pickings were first found in the Pyrenees and Warrandyte, then a cluey Californian veteran looked north in Clunes. Just over the ridge, in what was to become Ballarat, was the proverbial end of the rainbow. It wasn't long before miners were hauling 60lb (27kg) into Geelong at a time, and the rush was well and truly on.

The news spread around the world and brought hopefuls from Britain, Ireland, China, Germany, Italy, the USA and the Caribbean. By August 1852, 15,000 new arrivals docked in Melbourne each month. Crews jumped ship and hotfooted it to the diggings, stranding ships at anchor. Chaos reigned. Even if only for a night or two, everyone needed a place to stay and, when there was no room at the inns, stables were let for exorbitant amounts. Wives and children were often dumped in town while husbands continued on to the diggings. Governor La Trobe despaired of his grand civic vision as shanties and eventually a complete tent village sprung up. Canvas Town, on the south side of the Yarra, housed over 8000 people.

Catherine Spence, a journalist and social reformer, visited Melbourne at the height of the hysteria and primly observed 'this convulsion has unfixed everything. Religion is neglected, education despised…everyone is engrossed with the simple object of making money in a very short time'. Over 90% of Australia's £100 million gold haul in the 1850s was found in Victoria. The 20 million ounces found between 1851 and 1860 represented one-third of the world's total. That said, relatively few 'diggers' struck it lucky. The licensing system favoured large holdings, policing was harsh and scratching a living for many proved so difficult that it gave rise to dissent. For some, 1852 was indeed a golden year, but by 1854, simmering tensions exploded in Ballarat. Miners at the Eureka Stockade burnt their licences and a bloody conflict broke out against British officials. Under the banner of the Southern Cross, a motley multinational crew called for democratic reform and universal manhood suffrage, an ultimately quixotic act, but one that changed the face of Australian politics for good. Brotherhood, sadly, had its limits. The 40,000 miners who arrived from southern China to try their luck on the 'new gold mountain' were often targets of individual violence and, later, systemic prejudice. Regardless, the Chinese community has continued to be a strong and enduring presence in the city of Melbourne.

BOOM & CRASH

Gold brought undreamt-of riches and a seemingly endless supply of labour to Melbourne. Melbourne became 'marvelous Melbourne', one of the world's most beautiful Victorian-era cities, known for its elegance, as well as its extravagance. Grand expressions of its prosperous confidence include the **University of Melbourne** (Map pp104–5, E4), Parliament House (p40), the State Library of Victoria (p40) and the **Old Royal Mint** (Map pp36-7, C3; cnr William & La Trobe Sts). Magnificent public parks and gardens were planted. By the 1880s the city had become Australia's financial, industrial and cultural hub. The 'Paris of the Antipodes' claim was invoked; the city was flush with stylish arcades (as well as the odd flâneur, we're sure). The city spread eastwards and northwards over the surrounding flat grasslands, and southwards along Port Phillip. A public transport system of cable trams and railways spread into the suburbs.

In 1880, and again in 1888, the Melbourne International Exhibition was held, pulling well over a million visitors. The Royal Exhibition Buildings were constructed for this event; Melbourne's soaring paean to Empire and the industrial revolution is one of the few 19th-century exhibition spaces of its kind still standing. Sadly this flamboyant boast to the world was to be marvellous Melbourne's swan song.

In 1889, after years of unsustainable speculation, the property market collapsed and the decades that followed were a period of severe economic depression. Although Melbourne functioned as the capital of the new Federation of Australia from 1901 to 1927, the city's fortunes didn't really rally until after WWI, and by then its 'first city' status had been long lost to Sydney.

The enormity of Melbourne's losses during WWI can still be felt at the mournful **Shrine of Remembrance** (Map pp64–5, G1) in Kings Domain, and the city's revival in fortune during the 1920s was shortlived. The global depression of the 1930s again saw the city stagnate. With the outbreak of WWII, Melbourne became the hub of the nation's wartime efforts, and later the centre for US operations in the Pacific. It was boomtime again, though no time for celebration.

MODERN MELBOURNE

Close to a million non-British immigrants arrived in Australia during the 20 years after the war; at first Jewish refugees from eastern and central Europe, then larger numbers from Italy, Greece, the Netherlands, Yugoslavia, Turkey and Lebanon. (With the demise of blatantly racist 'white Australia' immigration policies in the early 1970s, many migrants from Southeast Asia were added to the mix.) Although the idea that Melbourne had ever been a purely Anglo-Celtic society is an anachronistic fantasy, the fact that a great proportion of migrants chose to live in Melbourne profoundly changed the city's cultural life. Melbourne's streets became vibrantly and irrevocably multicultural during this time and this diversity became an accepted, and treasured, way of life.

The postwar construction boom also irrevocably altered Melbourne's physical appearance, as new fringe suburbs were constructed to address the housing shortages brought on by sudden growth. Melbourne hosted the Olympic Games in 1956, and historic buildings were bulldozed with abandon as the city prepared to impress the world with its modernity.

REINVENTION

During the early 1970s a bourgeoning counterculture's experiments with radical theatre, drugs and rock 'n' roll rang out through the inner city, particularly in the then predominantly Italian neighbourhood of Carlton. By the late 1970s, Melbourne's reputation as a conservative 'establishment' city was further challenged by the emergence of a frantically subversive art, music and fashion scene that launched bands such as Nick Cave and the Bad Seeds onto the world stage. Like a hundred years before, land prices rose continuously throughout the 1980s and banks were queuing up to lend money to developers. Even the worldwide stock market crash in 1987 didn't slow things down, but in 1990 the property market collapsed, and Melbourne bore the full brunt of the recession.

Recovery was, this time, swift, and over the past decade Melbourne has been transformed; its urban redevelopment has embraced the waters of the Yarra River and Port Phillip Bay as well as the city. The previous (Labor) state government encouraged high-density living during this time, and the current government looks set to do the same: allowing main street high-rise development and pushing Melbourne's boundaries outwards to house its increasing population. The vibrant mix of ethnicities in the community continues to grow, with many recent immigrants from African nations and the Middle East.

THE ENVIRONMENT

Melbourne City Council has given a committment to reduce the city centre's greenhouse emissions to zero by 2020. This admirable strategy glosses over Victoria's reliance on brown-coal-fuelled electricity, although the state government has made some attempt to put the brakes on its rising emissions with research programs into (hopefully) green technologies. On the negative side, investment in public transport has been inadequate to deal with increased demand. Water shortages are an ongoing issue, with restrictions in force at the time of writing. These laws have prompted a complete rethink of the way in which water is used. Short showers and half-flush toilets have become a way of life for Melburnians, and many have also adopted household grey-water systems. Waste recycling is a success story: public rubbish bins often offer sorting chutes, and household waste can be presorted before collection.

GOVERNMENT & POLITICS

Melbourne is the capital of the state of Victoria, and the seat of the state's government. The **state parliament** (☎ 9651 8911; www.parliament.vic.gov

.au) meets in the imposing neoclassical Parliament House (p40) building on Spring St. There is a Legislative Council – the upper house – and a Legislative Assembly, or lower house. This state, or second level, of government is responsible for main roads, traffic management, public transport, policing, hospitals, education and most major infrastructure projects.

At the time of writing the Liberal Party was in government, led by Ted Baillieu. The Liberals won office in 2010 for the first time since losing to Labor's Steve Bracks in 1999. The new government raised more than a few hackles when it almost immediately allowed cattle to return to national parks to graze and announced that it would not follow its predecessors and phase out the polluting brown-coal power plant at Hazelwood.

The City of Melbourne, which takes in the city centre and its immediate surrounds, is governed by the **Melbourne City Council** (☎ 9658 9658; www.melbourne.vic.gov.au). At the time of writing, Robert Doyle, a former leader of the opposition in state parliament, was the mayor of Melbourne.

ON SCREEN

Melbourne's new Docklands movie production facilities copped a blow when the Australia dollar climbed to new highs, and it's still to be seen whether Melbourne can get back on the movie-making stage. And Melbourne looks good on the big screen. Filmmakers tend to eschew the stately and urbane and focus on the city's complex nature, from the whimsically suburban to the melancholic, grimy and gritty.

Some films to see:

The Story of the Kelly Gang (1906) Although only fragments remain of its original 70 minutes, what has survived of the world's first feature film is stylistically sophisticated. Shot in a St Kilda pharmacy and the upper Yarra suburbs of Heidelberg and Eltham, it features one of the Kelly gang's actual hand-wrought armour.

On the Beach (1957) Duck-and-cover-era drama with Melburnians facing the end of the world with an odd mix of partying and passivity. Sadly, not even Gregory Peck can save us. A train ride to Frankston will never be the same without Ava Gardner waiting at the other end.

Picnic at Hanging Rock (1975) Elliptical, sensual Australian New Wave classic; the rock of the title rises from the plains just beyond Melbourne's outer suburban fringe.

Pure Shit (1976) Called 'the most evil film ever made' by the *Herald* newspaper, this ultra lo-fi look at 24 hours in the life of four junkies has great shots of a still shambolic inner city as well as hilarious cameos from author Helen Garner, comedians Greig (HG Nelson) Pickhaver, Max Gillies and producer Bob Weis.

Mad Max (1979) Postapocalypse gangs take over the highways and the wide-screen anamorphic lens takes in Spotswood, Lara, Williamstown, a stunning car park underneath Melbourne Uni and the dunes of nearby Fairhaven.

Malcolm (1986) Set in the then working-class suburbs of Flemington and Preston, a quintessential Melbourne-eccentric story about a tram-obsessive turned petty crim. One of the first in a long line of suburban quirk flicks.

Dogs in Space (1986) Shot in the house in Richmond where director Richard Lowenstein had actually lived in the late '70s. The late Michael Hutchence is joined by a huge local ensemble cast in a swirling, chaotic chronicle of the city's punk past.

The Big Steal (1990) Ben Mendelsohn and Claudia Karvan charm in this home-grown teen movie with cars, scams and the good citizens of the western suburbs providing a comic backdrop.

Death in Brunswick (1991) Culture clash high farce with a witless outsider played by Sam Neill, set in a Greek restaurant in prehipster Brunswick. Nice supporting role by satirist John Clarke.

Romper Stomper (1992) Russel Crowe plays a violent, Nazi skinhead. Set in Footscray, this film's less-than-subtle depiction of Vietnamese-Australians feels rather too in line with the main protagonist's point of view.

The Castle (1997) Too many quotes to list here, but this triumph of good over evil has a spot in most Melburnians hearts (or the pool room).

Chopper (2000) Based on the life of not-so-petty but eternally charismatic criminal Mark Read. Eric Bana's portrayal of Collingwood's most infamous resident proved career-making.

The Bank (2001) Bank-bashing paranoid thriller with a rare appearance from corporate Melbourne *and* a Yarra water taxi.

Harvie Krumpet (2003) Oscar-winning claymation short made in Melbourne by local film-school grad Adam Elliot.

Ned Kelly (2003) Uneven, but thoughtful, depiction of Ned played by the late Heath Ledger, adapted from the novel *Our Sunshine*. Unlike Tony Richardson's troubled Mick Jagger vehicle, this one was shot in the actual locations.

Salaam Namaste (2005) Twisted tale of professional Indians abroad was the first Bollywood film shot entirely in Australia. Features loads of shiny city locales and stunning shots of Great Ocean Road beaches (and not forgetting the smash hit song 'My Dil Goes Mmm'...).

Kenny (2006) This mockumentary set in the western suburbs takes toilet humour to its logical conclusion and is a feature-length tribute to the vernacular flair of tradesmen.

Animal Kingdom (2010) Menacing and moodily beautiful, a crime family thriller that's fiction in name alone.

FURTHER READING
FICTION

The Mystery of a Hansom Cab (1886; Fergus Hume) Marvellous Melbourne–era crime fiction.
The Getting of Wisdom (1910; Henry Handel Richardson) Loss of innocence story set in a Melbourne girls' school; its simple direct style ushers in the 20th century.

Power Without Glory (1950; Frank Hardy) Barely fictionalised story of crime and politics in WWI Carringbush, a suburb closely resembling Collingwood.

Monkey Grip (1977; Helen Garner) Love gone wrong in the inner-city Melbourne of the '70s.

How to Make a Bird (2003; Martine Murray) For young adult readers, a country teenager's odyssey through St Kilda and Brunswick.

Players (2005; Tony Wilson) A satirical romp that skewers sporting celebrity and its media handmaidens.

The Time We Have Taken (2007; Steven Carroll) Luminous exploration of the radical changes of the 1970s and meditation on the rhythms of suburban life.

Sucked In (2007; Shane Maloney) The sixth of the Murray Whelan novels, which follow his journey through the ranks of a well-known but entirely fictional Australian political party and takes place firmly in Melbourne, a city he describes as 'on the way to nowhere'.

The Slap (2008; Christos Tsiolkas) Middle-class suburban life has never been so contentious.

NONFICTION & MEMOIR

Bearbrass (1995; Robyn Annear) Melbourne's first decades are brought vividly to life.

Australian Gothic: A Life of Albert Tucker (2002; Janine Burke) Midcentury Melbourne through the eyes of its artistic elite.

A City Lost and Found: Whelan the Wrecker's Melbourne (2005; Robyn Annear) The city's history is revealed in this fascinating story of the clash of progress and preservation.

Yarra (2005; Kristin Otto) An erudite but rollicking history of Melbourne's main waterway.

In My Skin (2006; Kate Holden) A personal story of heroin addiction and prostitution on the streets of St Kilda.

Unpolished Gem (2006; Alice Pung) A vivid story of immigration and moving from one culture to another.

Shadowboxing (2006; Tony Birch) Linked stories about a working-class childhood in 1960s Fitzroy.

Street Art Uncut (2006, Matthew Lunn) A visual narrative of the city's vibrant graffiti culture.

Thirteen Tonne Theory: Life Inside Hunters and Collectors (2008; Mark Seymour) The trials, triumphs and demise of one of Melbourne's most beloved rock bands.

How to Make Gravy (2010; Paul Kelly) Some 576 pages of memories from one of Melbourne's most articulate and moving lyricists.

DIRECTORY
TRANSPORT
ARRIVAL & DEPARTURE
AIR

Melbourne Airport

Often referred to as Tullarmarine or Tulla, **Melbourne Airport** (☎ 9297 1600; www.melbourneairport.com.au) is around 25km northwest of the city centre. The international and domestic terminals are within the same complex. There are no direct train or tram services linking the airport with the city. Taxis can be found on the ground floor outside each terminal; a ride to or from the city centre will take between 25 and 40 minutes and cost at least $40, plus an additional $2 airport parking fee for inward journeys.
Skybus (Map pp36-7, B5; ☎ 9335 3066; www .skybus.com.au; Southern Cross Station) runs a 24-hour shuttle between the city centre and the airport, with city

hotel drop-offs ($16/26 one way/ return) and, depending on traffic, takes around 25 to 35 minutes. All major car-hire companies are represented and the Tullamarine Fwy runs directly to Flemington, close to the city centre. The CityLink tollway forms part of the freeway. A 24-hour pass for the Tulla section costs $4.65, or $13.25 for Citylink (does not include Eastlink).

Avalon Airport

Some international and domestic flights operated by Jetstar and Tiger (at the time of writing, undergoing an extensive safety review), including some flights to and from Sydney and Brisbane, use **Avalon Airport** (☎ 5227 9100, 1800 282 566; www.avalonairport.com.au), around 55km southwest of the city centre.
Sunbus (Map pp36-7, B5; ☎ 9689 7999; www.sunbusaustralia.com.au) meets all flights at Avalon Airport and picks up or drops off at Southern Cross Station (50 minutes, $20/36 one

---

CLIMATE CHANGE & TRAVEL

Travel – especially air travel – is a significant contributor to global climate change. At Lonely Planet, we believe that all travellers have a responsibility to limit their personal impact. As a result, we have teamed with Rough Guides and other concerned industry partners to support Climate Care, which allows travellers to offset the greenhouse gases they are responsible for with contributions to energy-saving projects and other climate-friendly initiatives in the developing world. Lonely Planet offsets all staff and author travel.

For more information, turn to the responsible travel pages on www.lonelyplanet.com/ responsibletravel. For details on offsetting your carbon emissions and a carbon calculator, go to www.climatecare.org.

way/return). Book hotel pick-ups 48 hours prior to departure.

TRAIN & BUS
Southern Cross Station (Map pp36–7, B5) is Melbourne's main terminus for all regional rail and coach services operated by **V/Line** (☎ 9697 2076; www.vline.com.au), and Countrylink and Overland trains to Sydney and Adelaide respectively. The airport and many privately owned long-distance bus services also operate from this terminal.

BOAT
A car and passenger ferry, the **Spirit of Tasmania** (Map pp64-5, B4; ☎ 1800 634 906; www.spiritoftasmania.com.au), sails to Devonport on Tasmania's northern coast nightly from Station Pier (B4) in Port Melbourne, with additional day sailings during summer. The crossing takes around 11 hours.

VISA
Visas are required for all overseas visitors except for New Zealand nationals, who receive a 'special category' visa on arrival. Visa application forms are available from diplomatic missions, travel agents and the Australian **Department of Immigration and Citizenship** (☎ 13 18 81; www.immi.gov.au). Some visitors are eligible to apply for an online **Electronic Travel Authority** (www.eta.immi. gov.au).

CUSTOMS, DUTY FREE & TAX REFUND
Cash amounts of more than $10,000 and foodstuffs, goods of animal or vegetable origin must be declared at customs. **Australian Customs** (☎ 1300 363 263; www.customs .gov.au) screen bags for these items and this should be taken very seriously. Many other items can be brought in free of duty, provided that customs are satisfied they are for personal use. Travellers aged over 18 years have a duty-free quota of 2.25L of alcohol, 250 cigarettes and dutiable goods up to the value of $900 (or $450 for those under 18).

Australia has a 10% goods and services tax (GST) automatically applied to most purchases, though some fresh food items are exempt. If you purchase goods with a total minimum value of $300 from any one supplier within 30 days of departure from Australia, you're entitled to a GST refund. You can get a cheque refund at the designated booth located beyond Customs at Melbourne Airport. Contact the **Australian Taxation Office** (☎ 13 28 66; www.ato.gov.au) for details.

GETTING AROUND
Melbourne's city centre (the CBD) is a delight for visitors, with trams at the ready when you're fatigued

RECOMMENDED MODES OF TRANSPORT

	Flinders St Station	NewQuay, Docklands	St Kilda Rd, Southbank
Flinders St Station	n/a	Tram 7min	Walk 5min
NewQuay, Docklands	Tram 7min	n/a	Walk 15min, Tram 10min
St Kilda Rd, Southbank	Walk 5min	Walk 15min, Tram 10min	n/a
Brunswick St, Fitzroy	Walk 20min, Tram 10min	Tram 25min	Walk 25min, Tram 15min
Lygon St, Carlton	Walk 15min, Tram 5min	Tram 25min	Walk 20min, Tram 15min
Chapel St, South Yarra	Tram 15min, Train 10min	Tram 30min, Train 15min	Tram 15min
Fitzroy St, St Kilda	Tram 20min	Tram 25min	Tram 15min
Beaconsfield Pde, Albert Park	Tram 20min	Tram 15min	Tram 15min

or in a hurry. Surrounding areas can be reached easily via the extensive tram, train and bus network. All three methods of transport are overseen by **Metlink** (☎ 13 16 38; www.metlinkmelbourne.com.au).

The nearest bus/train/tram route or station is noted with 🚌 🚆 🚊 symbols in reviews in this book.

TICKETING

The myki ticketing system covers Melbourne's buses, trams and trains and uses a 'touch on, touch off' plastic card (adult $10 one-off

fee), available online (www.myki .com.au) and from **Flinders St Station** (Map pp36-7, F5), the **MetShop** (Map pp36-7, F4) and the Myki Discovery Centre at **Southern Cross Station** (Map pp36-7, B5). Myki cards can be topped up with cash at machines located at most stations (or online, though it can take 24 hours to process). If you're only in town for a few days, short-term Metcards can be bought from machines on buses, trains and trams, though fares are more expensive (Zone 1 myki two hour/daily $3.02/6.04,

Brunswick St, Fitzroy	Lygon St, Carlton	Chapel St, South Yarra	Fitzroy St, St Kilda	Beaconsfield Pde, Albert Park
Walk 20min, Tram 10min	Walk 15min, Tram 5min	Tram 15min, Train 10min	Tram 20min	Tram 20min
Tram 25min	Tram 25min	Tram 30min, Train 15min	Tram 25min	Tram 15min
Walk 25min, Tram 15min	Walk 20min, Tram 15min	Tram 15min	Tram 15min	Tram 15min
n/a	Walk 7min, Bus 2min	Tram 35min	Tram 30min	Tram 25min
Walk 7min, Bus 2min	n/a	Tram 30min	Tram 30min	Tram 20min
Tram 35min	Tram 30min	n/a	Tram 10min, Walk 20min	Tram 25min
Tram 30min	Tram 30min	Tram 10min, Walk 20min	n/a	Tram 7min, Walk 15min
Tram 25min	Tram 25min	Tram 20min	Tram 7min, Walk 15min	n/a

Metcard $3.80/7). The Metcard will be phased out by December 2012.

TRAM

Both iconic and useful, Melbourne's trams criss-cross the city and travel into the suburbs, from around 5am until midnight. Timetables are variable; expect a tram to rattle along roughly every five to 20 minutes. Travel in peak hour can require patience (and on some routes, a sense of the absurd), as delays and overcrowding are not uncommon. Light rail routes, such as the 96 from the city to St Kilda, are spared traffic snarls. As the tram lines tend to radiate out from the city, travel between suburbs can be tricky (buses fill these gaps).

Free W-class 'City Circle' trams trundle around the city perimeter (and into the depths of Docklands) from 10am to 6pm daily.

BIKE

Melbourne Bike Share (☎ 1300 711 590; www.melbournebikeshare.com.au) began in 2010 and has had a slow start than other cities around the world, mainly because of Victoria's compulsory helmet laws. Subsidised safety helmets can be bought in the city centre from 7-Eleven stores ($5 with a $3 refund). Each first half-hour of hire is free. Daily ($2.50) and weekly ($8) subscriptions require a credit card. The **Humble Vintage** (☎ 0432 032 450; www.thehumblevintage.com) rents out vintage bikes for around $30 per day (with helmet and lock).

BUS

Melbourne's red-and-yellow buses are usually of more use if travelling out into the suburbs, but can provide shortcuts on some inner routes. Many, but not all, are wheelchair (and stroller) accessible 'bendy' buses.

Melbourne City Council runs a free hop-on, hop-off tourist shuttle, from 9.30am and 4.30pm daily. The grey-and-red buses intersect with the City Circle Tram and travel beyond the grid to the Shrine of Remembrance, Carlton and the Arts Centre. Federation Sq's **visitor information centre** (Map pp36–7, F5; www.thatsmelbourne.com.au) has details.

TRAIN

Imposing Flinders St Station (Map pp36–7, F5) is the main terminal for all suburban trains. There are four other stations on the underground City Loop

route: Southern Cross, Flagstaff, Melbourne Central and Parliament. Handy for crossing the city, the loop stations connect with other routes; see station displays for details. Trains begin around 5am and finish at midnight and run roughly every 10 and 30 minutes, depending on the time of day. Sunday services begin a little later.

WATER TAXIS

Slow going but scenic **Melbourne Water Taxis** (Map pp36-7, E6; ☎ 0416 068 655; www.melbournewatertaxis.com. au) service the Yarra and Maribyrnong Rivers, from Southgate to Richmond or Williamstown.

TAXI

Melbourne's yellow taxis can be hailed, or look for one of the taxi ranks around the city, usually outside major hotels or at Flinders St and Southern Cross Stations. A fully shining rooftop light means the taxi is available. Finding one is not often a hassle, though this doesn't apply to rainy Friday nights, after midnight or New Year's Eve. The flagfall is $3.20, then it's $1.62 per kilometre. There's a 20% surcharge from midnight to 5am and fares must be prepaid between 10pm and 5am.

13 CABS (☎ 13 22 27)
Arrow (☎ 13 22 11)
Silver Top Taxis (☎ 13 10 08)

PRACTICALITIES
BUSINESS HOURS

Businesses and offices, including post offices, keep 9am to 5pm hours, Monday to Friday, with some larger post offices also open on Saturday mornings. Banks open at 9.30am and shut their doors at 4pm Monday to Thursday, and at 5pm on Friday. Retail hours tend to be a little later, usually 9.30am to 6pm, and shops often stay open until between 7pm and 9pm on Friday. Most shops also open on Saturday from 10am to 5pm and on Sunday from 11am or midday to 4pm or 5pm.

Pubs open from 11am to 1am; bars from 4pm to late. Restaurants open around noon to 3pm for lunch and then for dinner from 6pm to 10pm, and often close either on a Sunday or a Monday. That said, Melbourne bars, restaurants and cafes often blur their boundaries and many are all-day affairs, that will serve coffee and croissants at 7am and still be serving cocktails come midnight.

Banks, businesses and many shops are closed on public holidays (see p160). Museums and other attractions are closed on Good Friday, Christmas Day and Boxing Day.

CINEMA

Cinemas are spread throughout the city and suburbs and usually belong to the **Hoyts** (hoyts.com.au), **Dendy** (www.dendy.com.au), **Village** (www.villagecinemas.com.au) or **Greater Union** (www.eventcinemas.com.au) chains; see their websites for details. The days of truly independent cinemas are long gone, but for arthouse, foreign language and otherwise interesting flims try one of these:

Astor (Map p113, E1; ☎ 9510 1414; www.astor-theatre.com; cnr Chapel St & Dandenong Rd, St Kilda)

Cinema Nova (Map pp104-5, F5; ☎ 9347 5331; www.cinemanova.com.au; 380 Lygon St, Carlton)

Imax (Map pp104-5, G6; ☎ 9663 5454; www.imaxmelbourne.com.au; Melbourne Museum, 11 Nicholson St, Carlton)

Kino (Map pp36-7, H3; ☎ 9650 2100; www.dendy.com.au; 45 Collins St, City)

Palace Como (Map pp72-3, D3; ☎ 9827 7533; www.palacecinemas.com.au; cnr Toorak Rd & Chapel St, South Yarra)

Outdoor cinemas are popular in the summer; check their websites for seasonal opening dates and their program details.

Moonlight Cinema (www.moonlight.com.au; Gate D, Royal Botanic Gardens, Birdwood Ave, South Yarra)

Rooftop Cinema (www.rooftopcinema.com.au; Level 6, Curtin House, 252 Swanston St, City)

St Kilda Open Air Cinema (www.stkildaopenair.com.au; Sea Baths, 10-18 Jacka Blvd, St Kilda)

DISCOUNTS

Many attractions offer concession/child/family discounts. In this book they are listed accordingly.

ELECTRICITY

Power supply is 240V 50Hz. Plugs are three-pin, but different to the larger British sort. Universal adaptors are available from luggage and outdoor supply shops, department stores and some chemists.

EMERGENCIES

In the case of emergency, call ☎ 000, free from any phone, to be connected to the police, ambulance or fire brigade.

HOLIDAYS

New Year's Day 1 January
Australia Day 26 January
Labour Day First or second Monday in March
Good Friday & Easter Monday March or April
Anzac Day 25 April
Queen's Birthday Second Monday in June
Melbourne Cup Day First Tuesday in November
Christmas Day 25 December
Boxing Day 26 December

INTERNET

There's no shortage of internet cafes in Melbourne, and wi-fi access is increasingly common, both in public places as well as hotels. Several websites keep track of free wi-fi hotspots. **Only Melbourne** (www.onlymelbourne.com.au) has a comprehensive list, though we can't vouch for it's accuracy. Melbourne Airport offers wi-fi for a pay-as-you-go fee. Hotel rates vary from complimentary to ludicrously expensive daily fees, so it's best to check when booking. Expect to pay around $2 per hour at an internet cafe. Public libraries, including the State Library of Victoria, usually offer a free service but you'll probably need to book.

Useful online resources:
ABC Melbourne Podtours (www.abc.net.au/melbourne/) A great little series of podcasts that get under Melbourne's skin.
Lost and Found (www.visitvictoria.com/lostandfound) An e-newsletter with a focus on creative spaces and events from Visit Victoria, plus a FaceBook page with regular updates.
The Age (www.theage.com.au) Not just the daily news: Melbourne's broadsheet likes to keep up with what's going on in the way of entertainment, too.
Three Thousand (www.threethousand.com.au) Weekly newsletter with the very hottest tips on music, fashion, bars and other goings on around the city.
Missy Confidential (www.missyconfidential.com.au) Up-to-date details of all the retail sales.

LANGUAGE

Melbournians, along with most Australians, often issue forth with a colourful and sometimes baffling barrage of Australian English words, phrases, suffixes and pre-fixes. Although many people claim that there are discernable regional accents, linguistically it's hard to prove. Many people in Melbourne speak languages other than English; Greek, Italian, Vietnamese, Chinese, Turkish and Lebanese are the most common. There are certain terms that are Melbourne-specific, or traceable to the city.

Some specific terms:

bogan A person of little education or culture, the recent variation of 'cashed-up bogan' refers to the nouveau riche

buckley's A forlorn hope, no chance at all; thought to derive from the story of William Buckley, a convict escapee who was stranded when Victoria's first colony was abandoned

more front than Myers Bold; a reference to the large street frontage of the Myers department store

soov A souvlaki, usually uttered, and eaten, late at night

spana A spanakopita, a feta and spinach pastry

spekkie A spectacular mark, in AFL football

The Eastern The Eastern Freeway

The G The MCG

under the clocks Clocks mark the entrance to Flinders St Station; it's a familiar meeting place

MONEY

Australian dollars have 100 cents and coins come in denominations from 5c to $2. With five cents being the smallest unit of currency, cash transactions are rounded up or down. There are notes for $5, $10, $20, $50 and $100.

For exchange rates, see the inside front cover.

NEWSPAPERS, MAGAZINES & SPECIALIST GUIDES

Melbourne's broadsheet news-paper is the *Age* (www.theage.com .au), which covers local, national and international news. It has various supplements during the week, including the food-and-wine-focussed *Epicure* on Tuesday, and, on Friday, Melbourne's entertainment listing guide 'EG'. There's arts coverage on Saturday. It also carries Saturday and Sunday magazines, and a monthly city magazine titled *(melbourne) magazine*. The *Herald Sun* does what tabloids do well: several editions per day, scads of sensationalism and a whole lotta sport.

Most magazine publishing in Australia is cost-effective only with national circulation; several attempts to establish a Melbourne city magazine have failed. Some of this slack has been taken up by online ventures such as **Three Thousand** (www.threethousand.com.au). However, the current affairs and culture magazine, the *Monthly* (www.themonthly.com.au), the *Australian Book Review* (www .australianbookreview.com.au) and the charitable *Big Issue* (www .bigissue.org.au) are published locally so tend to be less Sydney-centric than some.

The excellent *Gourmet Traveller* (http://gourmettraveller.com.au) and *Vogue Entertaining and Travel* (www.vogue.com.au/in_vogue/vogue_entertaining_travel) magazines often have Melbourne restaurant news, features and reviews. The free *Melbourne's Child* (www.melbourneschild.com.au) magazine has listings of children's activities.

Music listings can be found in the free *Beat* (www.beat.com.au) and *Inpress* (http://streetpress.com.au) magazines.

The *Melbourne Design Guide* (edited by Viviane Stappmanns and Ewan McEoin), available at http://melbournedesignguide.com, is a great reference for visitors interested in the city's aesthetic side. The *Slow Guide Melbourne* (by Martin Hughes), which is available at www.slowguides.com.au, celebrates the local, natural, traditional and sensory, of which there is plenty in Melbourne.

ORGANISED TOURS

The free monthly *Me!bourne Events* guide, available at visitor information centres, hotels and newsagents, has a section on tours.

The National Trust publishes the *Walking Melbourne* ($20) booklet, which is particularly useful if you're interested in Melbourne's architectural heritage.

Some options:

Aboriginal Heritage Walk (Map pp82-3, B6; ☎ 9252 2429; www.rbg.vic.gov.au; Royal Botanic Gardens; adult/child $25/10; ⏱ 11am Tue & Thu & 1st Sun of the month) The Royal Botanic Gardens are on a traditional camping and meeting place of the original owners of the land, and this tour takes you through their story. The 1½-hour tour departs from the visitor centre.

Art Aficionado (☎ 0412 169 391; http://artaficionadotours.com; tours $70) Great way to pack in up to 13 of Melbourne's contemporary galleries/spaces in just a few hours.

City Circle trams (www.metlinkmelbourne.com.au/city _circle/routes.html) See p157 for details of this free service.

Hidden Secrets Tours (☎ 9663 3358; www.hiddensecretstours.com; tours from $95) Walking tours of around three hours that cover laneways, art and design or wine, with small groups and knowledgeable guides.

Kayak Tours (☎ 0418 106 427; www.kayakmelbourne.com.au; tours $99) Takes you past Melbourne's newest developments and explains the history of the older ones. Moonlight kayak tours are most evocative and include a fish 'n' chips dinner. Usually departs from wharf sheds on Victoria Harbour.

Maribyrnong River Cruises (☎ 9689 6431; www.blackbirdcruises.com.au; Wingfield St, Footscray; adult/child $20/5) Has a two-hour return cruise up the river to Avondale Heights departing daily at 1pm, or head the other way past Lonely Planet's head office on its one-hour cruise to Docklands (departs at 4pm;

adult/child $10/5). Both tours depart from the end of Wingfield St in Footscray.

Melbourne By Foot (☎ 1300 311 081; www.melbournebyfoot.com; tours $29) Take a couple of hours out with Dave and experience a mellow, informative walking tour that covers lane art, politics, and gives great insights into Melbourne's history and diversity.

Melbourne River Cruises (Map pp36-7, E6; ☎ 9681 32843 www.melbcruises.com.au) Docks at Gem Pier and travels up the Yarra River to Southgate. Ticket prices vary according to destination.

Walkin' Birrarung (☎ 8622 2600; www.koorieheritagetrust.com/education; $13) This unique two-hour walk explores both the landscape of the Yarra as well as the dramatic changes to both the Aboriginal people and the place. Highly recommended.

TELEPHONE

The increasingly elusive public payphone is either coin or card operated; local calls are on unlimited time and cost 50c, calls to mobile phones are timed and attract higher charges. Some payphones accept credit cards; many don't work at all. Local and international phonecards come in values ranging from $5 to $50 and are available in newsagents.

All Australian mobile-phone numbers have four-digit prefixes beginning with 04. Australia's digital network is compatible with GSM 900 and 1800 handsets. Quad-based US phones will also work. Prepaid SIM cards are available from providers such as **Telstra** (www.telstra.com), **Optus** (www.optus.com.au), **Virgin** (www.virginmobile.com.au) or **Vodafone** (www.vodafone.com.au).

USEFUL PHONE NUMBERS

Melbourne area code ☎ 03
Ambulance ☎ 000
Country code ☎ 61
Directory assistance ☎ 1223
International access code from Australia ☎ 0011
Local taxi ☎ 13 10 08
Police ☎ 000

TIPPING

It's common, but by no means obligatory, to tip in restaurants and upmarket cafes, if the service warrants it – a gratuity of between 5% and 10% of the bill is the norm. Taxi drivers will also appreciate you rounding up the fare, but there's no obligation to do this.

TOURIST INFORMATION

Melbourne's government-run **Visitor Information Centre** (Map pp36-7, F5; www.visitmelbourne.com; Federation Sq; 9am-6pm) provides an accommodation and tour service, and internet access. Its website is translated into several languages and offers some very comprehensive information. Its parent organisation **Tourism Victoria** (☎ 13 28 42; www.visitvictoria.com.au) has a phone service and website that are equally thorough. There are additional information booths located in the Bourke St Mall and at the international terminal at Melbourne Airport. Melbourne City Council's **That's Melbourne** (www .thatsmelbourne.com.au) is also an excellent resource.

TRAVELLERS WITH DISABILITIES

Many of Melbourne's attractions are accessible for wheelchairs. Trains and newer trams have low steps to accommodate wheelchairs and people with limited mobility. **Access Cabs** (☎ 13 62 94) and **Silver Top Taxis** (☎ 8413 7202) have wheelchair-accessible taxis; both should be booked ahead. Australian visitors can use their M50 cards and reciprocal taxi vouchers. Many car parks in the city have convenient spaces allocated for disabled drivers. All pedestrian crossings feature sound cues and accessible buttons.

The **Melbourne Mobility Centre** (Map pp36-7, G5; ☎ 9650 6499, TTY 9650 9316; www.accessmelbourne.vic.gov.au; 1st fl car park, Federation Sq; 🕑 9am-6pm Mon-Fri, 10am-4pm Sat-Sun) offers TTY phone and web services, equipment hire and general information including a mobility map, which can also be downloaded from the website. The **Travellers Aid Centres** (www.travel lersaid. org.au) are located at Flinders Street and Southern Cross Stations and provide assistance with special needs and offers a variety of facilities to travellers, including showers, baby-change facilities, toilets, lounge area, public telephone, lockers, stroller and wheelchair hire, ironing facilities, meeting-room hire and tourist information. There is another **branch** (Map pp36-7, B5; ☎ 9670 2873; Lower Concourse) at Southern Cross Station.

>INDEX

See also separate subindexes for See (p174), Shop (p176), Eat (p172), Drink (p172) and Play (p173).

000 map pages

⭐ **PLAY**
Amusement Parks

◉ SEE

000 map pages